Wishes, Lies, and Dreams

Other books by Kenneth Koch:

Wishes, Lies, and Dreams
Teaching Children to Write Poetry

by
Kenneth Koch
and
The Students of P.S. 61
in New York City

A Chelsea House Book

PERENNIAL LIBRARY
Harper & Row, Publishers
New York, Cambridge, Hagerstown, Philadelphia, San Francisco
London, Mexico City, São Paulo, Sydney

The photographs in this book are of Miss Jean Pitts' fifth-grade class, writing and reading poems about the ocean. They were taken at P.S. 61 in March 1970 by Helen Weaver.

This work was originally published by Chelsea House Publishers. It is here reprinted by arrangement.

First PERENNIAL LIBRARY edition published 1980.

ISBN: 0-06-080530-7

82 83 84 10 9 8 7 6 5 4 3 2

To Katherine Lappa
1902-1969

Contents

Acknowledgements

The children who wrote the poems in this book are the main ones I have to thank for its existence, but I am indebted to many adults as well. The teachers at P.S. 61 taught me much that I needed to know and helped in various ways to make my project of teaching in the school a success. Without Gert Wiener I never would have received the fourth-grade Wish Poems that led to some of the most important things I found out. I am also particularly indebted to Margaret Magnani, whose enthusiasm made possible the whole experience with her "N.E." class, and to Barbara Strasser, whose excitement about children writing poetry was communicated to her students in such an extraordinary way. Other teachers who helped me teach poetry were Les Bowman, Jacqueline Fischer, Diana Pilkington, Jean Pitts, Hannah Rodney, Carole Shapiro, and Priscilla Weick. The principal, Jacob Silverman, supported my project from the beginning and always made sure I had the freedom and mobility in the school that I needed.

Alvera Ampian and Betty Kray of the Academy of American Poets sponsored my first months of teaching at the school; later it was Teachers' and Writers' Collaborative—Sheila Murphy, Johanna Roosevelt, Joel Oppenheimer. Trudy Kramer (then Cater) of the New York City Parks Department's Cultural Affairs Division was a great help then and afterwards.

I also want to thank the Ingram-Merrill Foundation for a grant which helped me take time to work on this book, and the

Danforth Foundation, whose teaching award encouraged me greatly in completing it.

I had a lot of help in planning the book and in writing those parts of it I wrote. Helen Weaver, my editor at Chelsea House, has been enthusiastic and helpful with everything. The present form of the book is mainly the inspiration of Maxine Groffsky, who also described it in a letter in such a convincing way that I immediately had a publisher. With the writing I have had assistance from my wife, Janice, and from three friends who gave me careful critiques of my introductory essay—Emily Dennis, Ron Padgett, and James Schuyler.

To Ron Padgett I owe another, more obvious debt, since it was his inspired continuation of the poetry program at P.S. 61 that furnished this volume with a number of poems and ideas for poems. His performance also reassured me that the children's poems had not all been a dream, or a sort of artistic accident connected mysteriously to me. Using the method of poetry ideas, others could help children to write poetry too: it seemed worthwhile to put it in a book.

To Emily Dennis I owe not only a better introduction but also the major part of my interest in teaching children. Her children's art classes at the Metropolitan Museum and her work at Muse were an inspiration, as were the texts on art she wrote for the grade-school newspaper, *New York, New York*.

Katherine Lappa, to whom this book is dedicated, was my English teacher in Cincinnati in my junior year of high school. Without her I don't believe I would ever have written poetry. Or, if I had, it would have been much later and starting from much further back. She encouraged me to be free and deep and extravagant in what I wrote, so that I could find what was hidden in me that I had to say; and I think that now after all these years the main thing I have found to add to what she said was to say it to more children and to say it sooner. It is my greatest regret as I write this that she is not alive to see my book, which is so much hers.

New York City
January, 1970

KENNETH KOCH

Wishes, Lies, and Dreams

Teaching Children To Write Poetry

The Dawn of Me

I was born nowhere
And I live in a tree
I never leave my tree
It is very crowded
I am stacked up right against a bird
But I won't leave my tree
Everything is dark
No light!
I hear the bird sing
I wish I could sing
My eyes, they open
And all around my house
The Sea
Slowly I get down in the water
The cool blue water
Oh and the space
I laugh swim and cry for joy
This is my home
    For Ever

Jeff Morley, Fifth Grade, P.S. 61

Last winter and the spring before that I taught poetry writing to children at P.S. 61 on East 12th Street between Avenue B and Avenue C in Manhattan. I was sponsored first by the Academy of American Poets, then by the Teachers' and Writers'

Collaborative.* I was a special teacher, who, like an art teacher, took classes at certain times. I could vary these arrangements thanks to the sympathetic cooperation of Jacob Silverman, the principal, who helped me to see any class I liked, even on short notice. Unlike other special teachers, I asked the regular teacher to stay in the room while I was there; I needed her help and I wanted to teach her as well as the children. I usually went to the school two or three afternoons a week and taught three forty-minute classes. Toward the end I taught more often, because I had become so interested and because I knew I was going to write about it and wanted as much experience as possible. My interest in the whole subject originally was largely due to Emily Dennis and to her inspiring ways of teaching art to children at the Metropolitan Museum.

I was curious to see what could be done for children's poetry. I knew some things about teaching adults to write, for I had taught writing classes for a number of years at Columbia and the New School. But I didn't know about children. Adult writers had read a lot, wanted to be writers, and were driven by all the usual forces writers are driven by. I knew how to talk to them, how to inspire them, how to criticize their work. What to say to an eight-year-old with no commitment to literature?

One thing that encouraged me was how playful and inventive children's talk sometimes was. They said true things in fresh and surprising ways. Another was how much they enjoyed making works of art—drawings, paintings, and collages. I was aware of the breakthrough in teaching children art some

---

* Poetry teaching at P.S. 61 has been continued by Ron Padgett. I have also gone back a few times this year. In the summer of 1968, along with David Shapiro, I taught writing to children at Muse, the neighborhood museum in the Bedford-Stuyvesant section of Brooklyn, and some of what I say here is based on that experience, particularly the last part of Section III.

forty years ago. I had seen how my daughter and other children profited from the new ways of helping them discover and use their natural talents. That hadn't happened yet in poetry. Some children's poetry was marvelous, but most seemed uncomfortably imitative of adult poetry or else childishly cute. It seemed restricted somehow, and it obviously lacked the happy, creative energy of children's art. I wanted to find, if I could, a way for children to get as much from poetry as they did from painting.

I Ideas for Poems

My adult writing courses had relied on what I somewhat humorously (for its grade-school sound) called "assignments." Every week I asked the writers in the workshop to imitate a particular poet, write on a certain theme, use certain forms and techniques: imitations of Pound's *Cantos*, poems based on dreams, prose poems, sestinas, translations. The object was to give them experiences which would teach them something new and indicate new possibilities for their writing. Usually I found these adult writers had too narrow a conception of poetry; these "assignments" could broaden it. This system also made for good class discussions of student work: everyone had faced the same problem (translating, for example) and was interested in the solutions.

I thought this would also work with children, though because of their age, lack of writing experience, and different motivation, I would have to find other assignments. I would also have to go easy on the word "assignment," which wasn't funny in grade school. In this book I refer to assignments, poetry ideas, and themes; in class what I said was "What shall we write about today?" Or "Let's do a Noise Poem." My first poetry idea, a Class Collaboration, was successful, but after that it was a few weeks before I began to find other good ones. Another new problem was how to get the grade-school students excited about poetry. My adult students already were; but these children didn't think of themselves as writers, and poetry to most of them seemed something difficult and remote. Finding the right ideas for poems would help, as would working out the best way to proceed in class. I also needed poems to read to them that would give them ideas, inspire them, make them want to write.

I know all this now, but I sensed it only vaguely the first time I found myself facing a class. It was a mixed group of fifth and sixth graders. I was afraid that nothing would happen. I felt the main thing I had to do was to get them started writing, writing anything, in a way that would be pleasant and exciting for them. Once that happened, I thought, other good things might follow.

I asked the class to write a poem together, everybody contributing one line. The way I conceived of the poem, it was easy to write, had rules like a game, and included the pleasures without the anxieties of competitiveness. No one had to worry about failing to write a good poem because everyone was only writing one line; and I specifically asked the children not to put their names on their line. Everyone was to write the line on a sheet of paper and turn it in; then I would read them all as a poem. I suggested we make some rules about what should be in every line; this would help give the final poem unity, and it would help the children find something to say. I gave an example, putting a color in every line, then asked them for others. We ended up with the regulations that every line should contain a color, a comic-strip character, and a city or country; also the line should begin with the words "I wish."

I collected the lines, shuffled them, and read them aloud as one poem. Some lines obeyed the rules and some didn't; but enough were funny and imaginative to make the whole experience a good one—

I wish I was Dick Tracy in a black suit in England
I wish that I were a Supergirl with a red cape; the city of
    Mexico will be where I live.
I wish that I were Veronica in South America. I wish that I
    could see the blue sky . . .

The children were enormously excited by writing the lines and
even more by hearing them read as a poem. They were talking,
waving, blushing, laughing, and bouncing up and down. "Feelings at P.S. 61," the title they chose, was not a great poem, but
it made them feel like poets and it made them want to write
more.

I had trouble finding my next good assignment. I had found
out how to get the children started but didn't yet know how to
provide them with anything substantial in the way of themes or
techniques. I didn't know what they needed. I tried a few ideas
that worked well with adults, such as writing in the style of
other poets, but they were too difficult and in other ways in-
appropriate. Fortunately for me, Mrs. Wiener, the fourth
grade teacher, asked me to suggest some poetry ideas for her
to give her class. (I wasn't seeing them regularly at that time—
only the sixth graders.) Remembering the success of the Collaborations, I suggested she try a poem in which every line
began with "I wish." It had worked well for class poems and
maybe it would work too for individual poems, without the
other requirements. I asked her to tell the children that their
wishes could be real or crazy, and not to use rhyme.

A few days later she brought me their poems, and I was very
happy. The poems were beautiful, imaginative, lyrical, funny,
touching. They brought in feelings I hadn't seen in the children's poetry before. They reminded me of my own childhood
and of how much I had forgotten about it. They were all in-
nocence, elation, and intelligence. They were unified poems:
it made sense where they started and where they stopped. And
they had a lovely music—

I wish I had a pony with a tail like hair
I wish I had a boyfriend with blue eyes and black hair
    I would be so glad . . .

                      Milagros Diaz, 4*

Sometimes I wish I had my own kitten
Sometimes I wish I owned a puppy
Sometimes I wish we had a color T.V.
Sometimes I wish for a room of my own.
And I wish all my sisters would disappear.
And I wish we didn't have to go to school.
And I wish my little sister would find her nightgown.
And I wish even if she didn't she wouldn't wear mine.

                      Erin Harold, 4

    It seemed I had stumbled onto a marvelous idea for children's poems. I realized its qualities as I read over their work. I don't mean to say the idea wrote the poems: the children did. The idea helped them to find that they could do it, by giving them a form that would give their poem unity and that was easy and natural for them to use: beginning every line with "I wish." With such a form, they could relax after every line and always be starting up afresh. They could also play variations on it, as Erin Harold does in her change from "Sometimes" to "And." Just as important, it gave them something to write about which really interested them: the private world of their wishes. One of the main problems children have as writers is not knowing what to write about. Once they have a subject they like, but may have temporarily forgotten about, like wishing, they find

---

* Here, as elsewhere in this introduction, the number following the child's name indicates the grade he or she was in when the poem was written.

a great deal to say. The subject was good, too, because it encouraged them to be imaginative and free. There are no limits to what one can wish: to fly, to be smothered in diamonds, to burn down the school. And wishes, moreover, are a part of what poetry is always about.

I mentioned that I had told Mrs. Wiener to ask the children not to use rhyme. I said that to all my classes as soon as I had them start writing. Rhyme is wonderful, but children generally aren't able to use it skillfully enough to make good poetry. It gets in their way. The effort of finding rhymes stops the free flow of their feelings and associations, and poetry gives way to sing-song. There are formal devices which are more natural to children, more inspiring, easier to use. The one I suggested most frequently was some kind of repetition: the same word or words ("I wish") or the same kind of thing (a comparison) in every line.

Once I understood why the Wish Poem worked so well, I had a much clearer idea of what to look for. A poetry idea should be easy to understand, it should be immediately interesting, and it should bring something new into the children's poems. This could be new subject matter, new sense awareness, new experience of language or poetic form. I looked for other techniques or themes that were, like wishes, a natural and customary part of poetry. I thought of comparisons and then of sounds, and I had the children write a poem about each. As in the Wish Poems, I suggested a repetitive form to help give their poems unity: putting a comparison or a sound in every line. Devoting whole poems to comparisons and sounds gave the children a chance to try out all kinds, and to be as free and as extravagant as they liked. There was no theme or argument with which the sounds or comparisons had to be in accord: they could be experimented with for the pleasures they gave in themselves. In teaching painting an equivalent might be having children paint pictures which were only contrasting stripes or gobs of color.

In presenting these poetry ideas to the children I encouraged them to take chances. I said people were aware of many resemblances which were beautiful and interesting but which they didn't talk about because they seemed too far-fetched and too silly. But I asked them specifically to look for strange comparisons—if the grass seemed to them like an Easter egg they should say so. I suggested they compare something big to something small, something in school to something out of school, something unreal to something real, something human to something not human. I wanted to rouse them out of the timidity I felt they had about being "crazy" or "silly" in front of an adult in school. There is no danger of children writing merely nonsensical poems if one does this; the truth they find in freely associating is a greater pleasure to them—

A breeze is like the sky is coming to you . . .

Iris Torres, 4

The sea is like a blue velvet coat . . .

Argentina Wilkinson, 4

The flag is as red, white, and blue as the sun's reflection . . .

Marion Mackles, 3

Children often need help in starting to feel free and imaginative about a particular theme. Examples can give them courage. I asked my fourth graders to look at the sky (it was overcast) and to tell me what thing in the schoolroom it most resembled. Someone's dress, the geography book—but best of all was the blackboard which, covered with erased chalksmear, did look very much like it. Such question games make for an excited atmosphere and start the children thinking like poets. For the Noise Poem I used another kind of classroom example. I made some noises and asked the children what they sounded like. I crumpled up a piece of paper. "It sounds like paper." "Rain on the roof." "Somebody typing." I hit the chair with a ruler and asked what word that was like. Someone said "hit." What else? "Tap." I said close your eyes and listen again and tell me which of those two words it sounds more like, hit or tap. "It sounds more like tap." I asked them to close their eyes again and listen for words it sounded like which had nothing to do with tap. "Hat, snap, trap, glad, badger." With the primary graders * I asked, How does a bee go? "Buzz." What sounds like a bee but doesn't mean anything like buzz? "Fuzz, does, buzzard, cousin." The children were quick to get these answers and quick to be swept up into associating words and sounds—

A clink is like a drink of pink water . . .

Alan Constant, 5

A yoyo sounds like a bearing rubbing in a machine . . .

Roberto Marcilla, 6

Before they had experimented with the medium of poetry in this way, what the children wrote tended to be a little narrow and limited in its means—but not afterwards. Their writing quickly became richer and more colorful.

After the Comparison Poem and the Noise Poem, I asked my students to write a Dream Poem. I wanted them to get the feeling of including the unconscious parts of their experience

* At P.S. 61 some first and second grade classes are combined in one primary grade.

in their poetry. I emphasized that dreams didn't usually make sense, so their poems needn't either. Wishes and dreams are easy to doctor up so they conform to rational adult expectations, but then all their poetry is gone.

Their Dream Poems contained a surprising number of noises, and also comparisons and wishes—

> I had a dream of a speeding car going beep beep while a train
> went choo choo . . .
>
> *Ruben Luyando, 4*

> I dream I'm standing on the floor and diamonds snow on me.
> I dream I know all the Bob Dylan songs my brother knows . . .
>
> *Annie Clayton, 4*

My students, it was clear, weren't forgetting things from one poem to the next; they had been able to write more vivid poems about their dreams because of the other poems they had recently written. To encourage them in combining what they knew, I next asked them to write a poem deliberately using wishes, noises, comparisons and dreams all together.

The Metaphor Poem, which I had the fourth graders write next, was a variation of the Comparison Poem, and more difficult than it, probably because it isn't as natural to children to make metaphors as to make comparisons; metaphors require an extra act of thought. Some children wrote Metaphor Poems and many wrote new Comparison Poems. Something of this kind which the children found easier was the Swan of Bees Poem, which required in every line not a *like* or an *as,* as in the Comparison Poem, but an *of.* The idea was to put in every line a strangely composed object, like a swan of bees. "Swan of bees" was a spelling mistake a third grader made in his Comparison Poem: he meant to write "swarm" but wrote "swan" instead. Believing that his error had created something interesting and beautiful, I wanted to share it with the class; I was pleased to have a live example of the artistic benefits that can come from error and chance. The children seemed to find the swan of bees as beautiful as I did, and when I proposed they write a poem full of such things they responded enthusiastically. Being able to create things out of no matter what suggested marvelous possibilities—

> I have a sailboat of sinking water
> I was given a piece of paper made of roses . . .
>
> *Eliza Bailey, 3*

> I had a dream of my banana pillow
> And of my pyjamas of oranges . . .
>
> *Madelyn Mattei, 3*

This was only one of many poetry ideas I had which were directly inspired by the children's work. After my students had written a few basic poems like Comparisons, Wishes, and Noises, I began to be guided more by my sense of where they were in their development as poets and what they might be ready for next.

A poetry theme that all my classes were ready for at this point was the contrast between the present and the past. To give their poems form and to help them get ideas, I suggested that they begin every odd line with I Used To and every even line with But Now. Like Wishes and Dreams, this poem gave the children a new part of experience to write about. It gave them a chance too to bring in comparisons, dreams, and other things they had learned—

I saw a red doll and feel I am red
But that was a dream . . .

> *Thomas Kennedy, 3*

I used to be a baby saying Coo Coo
But now I say "Hello" . . .

> *Lisa Smalley, 3*

I used to have a teacher of meanness
But now I have a teacher of roses . . .

> *Maria Ippolito, 3*

Some of the content brought into their poetry by this theme surprised me. Among the primary and third graders metempsychosis was almost as frequent a theme as the conventionally observed past:

I used to be a fish
But now I am a nurse . . .

> *Andrea Dockery, 1*

I used to be a rose but now I'm a leaf
I used to be a boy but now I'm a woman
I used to have a baby but now he's a dog . . .

> *Mercedes Mesen, 3*

I used to be a design but now I'm a tree . . .

Ilona Baburka, 3

I had forgotten that whole strange childhood experience of changing physically so much all the time. It came very naturally into the children's poems once I found a way of making it easy for them to write about change—that is, by suggesting the pattern I Used To/But Now.

I gave other assignments in my first two months at P.S. 61, but these were the ones that worked out best. Each gave the children something which they enjoyed writing about and which enabled them to be free and easy and creative. Each also presented them with something new, and thus helped them to have, while they were writing, that feeling of discovery which makes creating works of art so exhilarating. The success of these particular assignments, as well as of some I gave later, was due partly to their substance and partly, I think, to the accident of my finding an effective way to present them. A child's imagination can be reached in many ways. Some ideas that didn't turn out so well, such as a poem about mathematics, would doubtless have worked better if I had been able to find a way to make them suggestive and exciting. In these first poems, in any case, I thought the children had come to like poetry, and had become familiar with some of the basic themes and techniques that make it so enjoyable to write.

The repetition form, which I often suggested they use, turned out to have many advantages. Repetition is natural to children's speech, and it gave them an easy-to-understand way of dividing their poems into lines. By using it they were able to give strong and interesting forms to their poems without ever sounding strained or sing-song, as they probably would have using rhyme. And it left their poetry free for the kind of easy and spontaneous music so much appreciated by contemporary poets, which rhyme and meter would have made impossible—

21

I wish planes had motors that went rum bang zingo and would
be streaming green as the sea . . .

Argentina Wilkinson, 4

One of the saddest things are colors because colors are sad and
roses are sad two lips are sad and having dates is sad too
but the saddest color I know is orange because it is so
bright that it makes you cry . . .

Mayra Morales, 3

Children can be fine musicians when the barriers of meter and
rhyme aren't put in their way.

Another strategy I'd used more or less instinctively, encouraging the children to be free and even "crazy" in what they wrote,
also had especially good results. They wrote freely and crazily
and they liked what they were doing because they were writing
beautiful and vivid things. The trouble with a child's not
being "crazy" is that he will instead be conventional; and it is
a truth of poetry that a conventional image, for example, is not,
as far as its effect is concerned, an image at all. When I read
"red as a rose," I don't see either red or a rose; actually such
a comparison should make me see both vividly and make me see
something else as well, some magical conjunction of red and
rose. It's another story when I read "orange as a rose" or even
"yellow as a rose"—I see the flower and the color and something beyond. It is the same when one writes as when one reads:
creating in himself the yellow and the rose and the yellow rose
naturally gives a child more pleasure and experience than repeating a few words he has already heard used together. As I
hope I've made clear, the best way to help children write freely
is by encouragement, by examples, and by various other inspiring means. It can't be done by fiat, that is, by merely telling
them to be "imaginative and free."

The best poetry assignments I found in my second stint at P.S. 61 (December 1968 to February 1969), like these first ones, added something new to what the children could write about and did it in a way that interested and excited them. My first December visit to the school was during a snowstorm, and I thought there would be considerable sentiment for a snow poem. To help the children avoid wintry Christmas-card clichés I proposed that instead of writing about the snow they write as if they were the snow, or rather the snowflakes, falling through the air. I said they could fall anyplace they liked and could hurt and freeze people as well as make them happy. This made them quite excited. Children are so active and so volatile that pretending to be something can be easier for them than describing it—

> If I were the snow I would fall on the ground so the children
> could pick me up and throw me into the air . . .
>
> *Ana Gomes, 6*

> We would cover the sun with clouds so it could not melt
> us . . .
>
> *Carmine Vinciforo, 6*

Later they wrote poems about animals and objects, and for these poems too I suggested that they be the animal or object rather than describe it—

> I'm the floor of a house. Everytime someone steps on me I
> laugh . . .
>
> *Billy Constant, 4*

A Lie Poem worked out very well. I asked the children to say something in every line which wasn't true, or to simply make the whole poem something not true. I know "lie" is a strong word; I used it partly for its shock value and partly because it's a word children use themselves. "Fantasy" is an adult word and "make-believe" has fairytale and gingerbread associations that I wanted to avoid. The Lie Poem, like the Wish and Dream Poems, is about how things might be but really aren't—though, as in Jeff Morley's "The Dawn of Me," it can lead to surprising truths.

Color Poems—using a different color in every line, or the same color in every line—were a great hit. The children had been using colors in their poems all along and they liked devoting whole poems to them—

> Yellow, yellow, yellow. The sky is yellow. The streets are
> yellow. It must be a yellow day . . .
>
> *Elizabeth Cabán, 5*

I also had the children write poems while listening to music. The school had a phonograph on which I played for my different classes records by De Falla, Ravel, Mozart, and Stravinsky, while they wrote images and lines which the music suggested to them. The immediacy of the music, like that of the snowstorm earlier, was inspiring—

> This whole world appears before me.
> I wish to soar like a bird in the yellow-green sky . . .
>
> *Ruben Marcilla, 6*

> I was looking at the sun and I saw a lady dancing and I saw
> myself and I kept looking at the sun then it was getting to

be nighttime then the moon was coming up and I kept
looking at it it was so beautiful . . .

Ileana Mesen, 4

My fifth grade class wrote two sestinas. The sestina is a
seemingly difficult form, but actually the only hard thing about
it is remembering the order in which the six end-words are
repeated. I did the sestina as a class collaboration: I wrote
the end-words, in proper order, on the blackboard, and asked
the students for lines to fit them. This way the children got
the pleasure of solving the puzzle aspect of the poem—making
their lines and ideas fit the form—without the troublesome
remembering part. The sestina taught the children something
new about the poetic possibilities of repeating individual words.
Erin Harold's "Gardentail," which was written a week later, I
think shows its influence:

Gardenia's walking over Nellie
And Gardenia is a mouse
Her tail's still over Nellie
Who would rather step on tail
Gardenia's walking through the grass
But her tail is still on Nellie
Gardenia's going uphill
Gardenia's going downhill
She's wading through a stream . . .

Erin Harold, 5

There are other strict forms—the pantoum, for example—which
could be made easy for children to write and would teach them
something they would enjoy using in other poems.

A poetry idea which, like I Used To / But Now, brought a
new part of their experience into the children's poetry, was one
about the difference between how they seemed to other people
and how they felt they really were. I suggested a two-line repeating form, as in the Used To Poem: I Seem To Be / But
Really I Am. The sixth graders were particularly affected by
this theme, being at an age when private consciousness and
social image are sometimes seriously different. For one thing,
there are hidden sexual and romantic feelings which one
doesn't confess—

> I seem to be shy when she passes by but inside of me I have a
> wonderful feeling . . .
> As we went for a walk in the park I felt a wet kiss hit my dry
> skin.

> *Robert Siegel, 6*

Other contrasting themes I thought of but haven't yet tried
are I Used To Think / But Now I See (or Know); I Wish /
But Really; I Would Like / But I Would Not Like.

I asked my students to write poems using Spanish words,
which delighted the Spanish-speaking children and gave the
others an experience of the color and texture of words in another language. I chose Spanish because so many children at
P.S. 61 speak it, and I wanted them to be able to enjoy their
knowledge of it. There is such emphasis in the schools on teaching Spanish-speaking children correct English that the beauties
and pleasures of the Spanish language are usually completely
forgotten. I chose twenty Spanish words in advance, wrote them
on the board, and asked the children to include most of them
in their poems. This worked out best in the fifth-grade class,
where I asked the students to invent a new holiday (it was near
Christmas) and to use the Spanish words in describing its main
features—

On my planeta named Carambona La Paloma
We have a fiesta called Luna Estrella . . .
We do a baile named Mar of Nieve . . .

Marion Mackles, 5

. . . the estrellas are many colors
And the grass is verde.

Esther Garcia, 5

The children were not limited to the words I wrote on the board; I told them they could write their whole poem in Spanish, and some did.

The best assignments to begin with, I think, are Class Collaborations, Wishes, Comparisons, Noises, Lies, and Colors. Children are excited by all of them, and each can show them some of the special pleasures of poetry. Many other assignments are possible, of course, aside from the ones I've described. Among those Ron Padgett used at the school were collaborative poems by two students and poems about what you could see with a third eye. At Muse, David Shapiro had the children write poems while he played the violin; another time he borrowed a white mouse from the Muse live animal collection and had each child hold it in his hand and then write a poem about what it would be like to be a mouse. The success of any assignment depends upon how one goes about presenting it and more generally how one approaches the whole subject of teaching children to write.

II Teaching Children to Write Poetry

Some things about teaching children to write poetry I knew in advance, instinctively or from having taught adults, and others I found out in the classroom. Most important, I believe,

28

is taking children seriously as poets. Children have a natural talent for writing poetry and anyone who teaches them should know that. Teaching really is not the right word for what takes place: it is more like permitting the children to discover something they already have. I helped them to do this by removing obstacles, such as the need to rhyme, and by encouraging them in various ways to get tuned in to their own strong feelings, to their spontaneity, their sensitivity, and their carefree inventiveness. At first I was amazed at how well the children wrote, because there was obviously not enough in what I had told them even to begin to account for it. I remember that after I had seen the fourth-grade Wish Poems, I invited their teacher, Mrs. Wiener, to lunch in order to discover her "secret." I thought she must have told her students certain special things to make them write such good poems. But she had done no more than what I had suggested she do: tell the children to begin every line with "I wish," not to use rhyme, and to make the wishes real or crazy. There was one other thing: she had been happy and excited about their doing it and she had expected them to enjoy it too.

I was, as I said, amazed, because I hadn't expected any grade-school children, much less fourth graders, to write so well so soon. I thought I might have some success with sixth graders, but even there I felt it would be best to begin with a small group who volunteered for a poetry workshop. After the fourth-grade Wish Poems, however, and after the Wish and Comparison Poems from the other grades, I realized my mistake. The children in all the grades, primary through sixth, wrote poems which they enjoyed and I enjoyed. Treating them like poets was not a case of humorous but effective diplomacy, as I had first thought; it was the right way to treat them because it corresponded to the truth. A little humor, of course, I left in. Poetry was serious, but we joked and laughed a good deal; it

29

was serious because it was such a pleasure to write. Treating them as poets enabled me to encourage them and egg them on in a non-teacherish way—as an admirer and fellow worker rather than as a boss. It shouldn't be difficult for a teacher to share this attitude once it is plain how happily and naturally the students take to writing.

There are other barriers besides rhyme and meter that can keep children from writing freely and enjoying it. One is feeling they have to spell everything correctly. Stopping to worry about spelling a word can cut off a fine flow of ideas. So can having to avoid words one can't spell. Punctuation can also be an interference, as can neatness. Good poetic ideas often come as fast as one can write; in the rush to get them down there may be no time for commas or for respecting a margin. All these matters can be attended to after the poem is written.

Another barrier is a child's believing that poetry is difficult and remote. Poetry should be talked about in as simple a way as possible and certainly without such bewildering rhetorical terms as *alliteration*, *simile*, and *onomatopoeia*. There are easy, colloquial ways to say all these: words beginning with the same sound, comparisons using *like* or *as*, words that sound like what they mean. Poetry is a mystery, but it is a mystery children can participate in and master, and they shouldn't be kept away from it by hard words.

Again on the subject of language, the various poetry ideas should be presented in words children actually use. I don't think the Wish Poems would have been so successful if I had asked my students to start every line with "I desire." Nor would "My seeming self" and "My true self" have worked well in place of "I Seem To Be / But Really I Am." One should be on the lookout, too, for words and phrases which tell the child what to say and take him away from important parts of his experience: I think "make-believe" and "imaginary" are such words. When I told a teacher at another school about the "I wish" assignment, she said that she had done almost the same thing but it hadn't turned out as well. She had had her students write poems in which every line began with "Love is." I never heard a child say "love is" in my life, and so I wasn't surprised that they hadn't responded wholeheartedly.

One bar to free feeling and writing is the fear of writing a bad poem and of being criticized or ridiculed for it. There is also the oppression of being known as not one of the "best." I didn't single out any poems as being best or worst. When I read poems aloud I didn't say whose they were, and I made sure that everyone's work was read every so often. If I praised a line or an image I put the stress on the kind of line or image it was and how exciting it might be for others to try something like that too. That way, I felt, the talent in the room was being used for the benefit of everyone.

The teacher shouldn't correct a child's poems either. If a word or line is unclear, it is fine to ask the child what he meant, but not to change it in order to make it meet one's own standards. The child's poem should be all his own. And of course one shouldn't use a child's poetry to analyze his personal problems. Aside from the scientific folly of so doing, it is sure to make children inhibited about what they write.

A surprising discovery I made at P.S. 61 was that children enjoyed writing poems at school more than at home. I had assumed that like grownup writers they would prefer to be comfortable, quiet, and alone when they wrote, but I was wrong. Once it had to be done away from school, poetry was part of the detestable category "homework," which cuts one off from the true pleasures of life; whereas in school it was a welcome relief from math, spelling, and other required subjects. Closing their heavy books to hear about a new idea for a poem made the children happy and buoyant. There was also the fact of their all being there in the room, writing together. No time for self-consciousness or self-doubts; there was too much activity: everyone was writing and talking and jumping around. And it was competitive in a mild and exhilarating way: it was what everyone was doing and everyone could do it.

The children wrote a few lines, showed them to each other, copied, teased, called to me for help or admiration, and then went back to their writing. Out of this lovely chaos, after fifteen minutes or so, finished poems would begin to appear, handed to me written in pencil on sheets of notebook paper, that would make me gasp. That is how almost all these poems were composed. The classroom was so drab-looking and so noisy, with the students talking, the PA system going BOOP BOOP and the trash can going BOOM (during many a writing session it was rolled in and out of the room), that I couldn't imagine sitting there and writing a poem. The children, however, seemed not to be distracted at all.

I let the children make a good deal of noise. Children do when they are excited, and writing poetry is exciting. I let them change papers and read each other's poems too. Sometimes in that maelstrom of creation one student's idea would seem so irresistible that another would use it. But not many lines were stolen, and the poetry thief always went on to something of his own.

One important advantage to writing in class was that I was there: before the children wrote, to explain and to inspire; and while they were writing, to act as reader, admirer, and furnisher of additional ideas. It is true that I could have explained an assignment and let the children carry it out at home. What I couldn't have done was keep the new idea and their excitement about it fresh in their minds from noon till seven-thirty, or whenever they would sit down to write. For each poem I did certain things and gave certain examples to help make the idea clear and to put the children in the mood for writing. In giving the Color Poem, for instance, I asked them to close their eyes; then clapped my hands and asked them what color that was. Almost everyone raised his hand: "Red!" "Green!" "White!" I asked them what color Paris was; London; Rome; Los Angeles. I told them to close their eyes again and I said certain words and certain numbers, asking them what color those were. The point was to get them to associating colors freely with all kinds of things before writing the poem. Almost always a part of my preparation was reading other children's poems aloud, and the effect of these was most vivid when the class wrote immediately after hearing them.

I could also be helpful to the children while they were actually writing. Often students got the feeling when they were about to start writing that they didn't really understand the assignment, so they would call me over to make it clearer. Sometimes a student would be stuck, unable to start his poem. I would give him a few ideas, while trying not to give him actual lines or words—"Well, how do musical instruments sound? Why don't you write about those?" or "What do you hear when you're on a boat?" Sometimes students would get stuck in the middle of a poem, and I would do the same sort of thing. Sometimes I would be called over to approve what had been written so far, to see if it was OK. I often made such comments as "That's good, but write some more," or "Yes, the first three lines in particular are terrific—what about some more like that?" or "That's not exactly what I meant. Turn it over; let's start again," or "I think maybe it's finished. What about another poem on the other side?"

So I was useful in the classroom for getting the children in a good mood to write and then for keeping them going. And they were useful to each other in creating a humming and buzzing creative ambiance. They helped and inspired each other as well by the poetry they wrote, which afterwards everyone could read or hear. I have already mentioned my practice of reading aloud to one class the poems of another. Once I had discovered the various good effects of doing this, it became an important part of my teaching.

By listening to or reading poems, children can become excited about writing and can learn new ideas and techniques. Aware of the value of poetry for inspiring and teaching poets, I looked around for the right poems to use at P.S. 61. It wasn't easy. The children responded to adult poetry with interest and intelligence; my grade-school students enjoyed the work of even the obviously difficult modern poets I read to them—Dylan Thomas, Theodore Roethke, John Ashbery. But adult poetry— even that of Whitman and other apparently easier writers—was too distant from the way they thought, felt, and spoke to touch them in so immediate a way that they wanted to write similar poems of their own. A hasty look at and a long memory of poetry for children by adults showed me that it was not what I wanted either. It was too often condescending and cute and almost always lacked that clear note of contemporaneity and relevance, both in subject and in tone, which makes the work of a writer's contemporaries so inspiring to him. The best poems I found to read, finally, were those that the children at P.S. 61 were writing. I didn't have any that would serve until the fourth graders wrote their Wish Poems. When I saw these I decided to try them out on the primary class. It was my first visit to this class, in which the students were from six to eight years old.

I had really been delighted by these poems, but the response of the primary graders was even wilder and happier than my own. There were about forty of them, seated at their desks

34

arranged in a large U-formation, all looking up at me and wondering what was going on. They hadn't seen a "poetry teacher" before. When I started to read the fourth-grade Wish Poems, it was as though they couldn't believe what was happening. Their secret thoughts and dreams, cast into verse, and being read to them in school by a smiling man! How could anybody have found out such things?

> I wish I could leap high into the air and land softly on my toes.
> I wish I could dance in every country in the world . . .
>
> *Melanie Popkin, 4*

> I wish I had a kitten to do my homework
> And a chimpanzee to do my housework . . .
>
> *Ruby Johnson, 4*

Within a few moments, first a few students and then the whole class was shouting "Yeah!" at the top of their lungs after every wish, that is, after every line of every poem. The commotion was tremendous. The fourth graders' poems really moved them, and they were bursting with ideas for poems of their own. I hadn't been sure that children so young would be able to write anything, but paper was passed out and they immediately wrote one-line Wish Poems (to warm up) and a little later they wrote longer ones. Their handwriting was clumsy and their spelling uncertain, but what they had to say and how they said it were something else—

> I wish me and my brother and my friend Paul were birds . . .
>
> *David Jeanpierre, 1*

> I wish I was soso, and I wish I was bobo too. I wish I was a
> book so the children could read me . . .

Zaida Rivera, 1

I read some fourth grade poems to my other classes too, with
equally good, if less extravagant, effects.

Once this got started I was reading poems from all grades to
all other grades. The primary graders wrote the first Used To /
But Now Poems, and children in the other classes were excited
by lines like Andrea Dockery's

> I used to be a fish
> But now I am a nurse . . .

Some children took over her idea and made something of it for
themselves—

> I used to be a goldfish
> But now I am a girl . . .

Lisa Smalley, 3

or, in a crazier vein—

> I used to be a nurse
> But now I am a dead person
> I always was Mr. Coke
> But now I am Mrs. Seven Up . . .

Thomas Rogaski, 3

The younger children's feeling for physical transformation
was doubtless the emotional source of these lines, but I think

Andrea's couplet was the literary influence that made possible its expression. Often other children's poetry would not only excite my students and make them want to write but would also, as in this case, suggest particular techniques or variations on a theme. Of course these two effects aren't really separate, since an artist tends to appropriate to some extent that part of someone else's work which inspires him. I wasn't concerned that the children would slavishly imitate each other and so be constricted rather than instructed. I felt that my attitude toward their writing would help prevent that, as well as their own strong inclination to make things of their own.

It was soon clear that it wasn't copying that was going on but something more like the usual artistic process of learning through influence and imitation. The poetry written at P.S. 61 was their poetry, as twentieth-century American poetry is mine. When they were older, that larger literature would be theirs too, but now, though it interested them, it was too difficult and full of adult attitudes for them to feel close to it. The works of their exact contemporaries who were writing on the same subjects were another matter. Images, lines, and ideas in one poem, if they were good ones, carried by my voice across the room, would instantly begin to blossom in new places, changed by the personality of the writer, and usually just as fresh and new as they had been before. For example, many students learned from Erin Harold's poem about her sisters how to express aggressive feelings toward siblings, parents, and friends without feeling bad about it. It wasn't the substance they learned, but how to deal with it in a light-hearted yet convincing way. Another influential poem was Mary Minn's Comparison Poem, which gave others an example of talking about one sense in the language of another—

Snow is as white as the sun shines.
The sky is as blue as a waterfall.
A rose is as red as a beating of drums.
The clouds are as white as the busting of a firecracker.
A tree is as green as a roaring lion.

Mary Minns, 4

In Gloria Peters' "What's Like What," there are images very close to Mary Minns'—

Black is as black as a drum thumping
But red is as red as a firecracker cracking . . .

and others in which the same technique is used to do something quite original—

But white is as white as screaming out
The rain is as pink as pink tears
But orange is as orange as a blunk
That's What's Like What!

Gloria Peters, 5

I was learning from their poems also. Having the children associate colors and sounds as preparation for the Color Poems and the Poems Written To Music was an idea I got from Mary Minns' poem and others like it. We were, the students and I, creating something like a literary tradition, and everyone could learn and profit from it. It was not only poems written for the same assignment that I read to my classes. Colors had turned up before the Color Poem, and I read some poems in which they had occurred when I presented that assignment. Sometimes it was just an interesting turn of phrase or kind of verbal music that I wanted my students to hear.

So hearing and reading other students' poems inspired the children, made them want to write, gave them new ideas. Having seen how the children were affected by these P.S. 61 poems, I thought harder about how to bring in some of the great poetry of the past and present so that they could learn from it and be inspired by it in similar fashion. They were getting some knowledge of that poetry indirectly through me, since it was, after all, the substance of what I knew about poetry; but I wanted them to feel the force of a poet like Whitman or Wallace Stevens directly. My early classes at the school had shown me it wasn't enough merely to read them this poetry. But now I knew a few things from reading them their own poems: that they were particularly attentive to poetry just before they were going to write, and that if the poem I read had something to do with what they were going to write about, their interest in and absorption of it was increased. I thought this would be true even if the poem was a little hard for them. So what I had to do was find poems or parts of poems that fitted in with my assignments, or else begin with a poet's work and find a way to make an assignment out of one of its characteristics. By reading or hearing the poet's work before they wrote their own poems on a similar theme, they could enjoy it and learn from it; some of its remoteness would be removed by its being a part of something they themselves were going to do. Wallace Stevens' "Bantams Among Pine Woods" would be a part of one of their activities rather than something apart from them which they were to analyze, appreciate, or describe. Just as it is easier and more natural for children to write as if they *were* the snow than it is for them to describe it, so it is easier for them to participate in a difficult poem (that is, enjoy it, get lost in it, be moved and influenced by it) than to describe or criticize it. It is a little hard to believe at first that a ten-year-old child who might not be able to say one thing about Stevens' poetry could catch and reproduce its music in an original way. Some of my fourth graders did that, though, in their Noise Poems, for which part of the preparation had been my reading aloud "Bantams" and other poems from *Harmonium*—

> Owl go like who and who. Who and who and who . . .
>
> *Maria A. Rivera, 4*

> The rock and roll. Roll rock came ricking and rocking to
>   rock . . .
>
> *Eduardo Diaz, 4*

> The sun had the glare of glass in it . . .
>
> *Annie Clayton, 4*

This was a case of finding some part of a poet's work which fitted an assignment I already had in mind. It was the same when, for the Color Poem, I read aloud de la Mare's "Silver," Dylan Thomas's "Fern Hill," and, in my terrible Spanish, Lorca's "Romance Sonambulo" (*"Verde que te quiero verde . . ."*), with a rough English translation.

D. H. Lawrence's poetry seemed to me likely to be interesting and appealing to my students—the free verse poems of *Birds, Beasts and Flowers* and *Pansies*, both for their subjects and for their simple conversational tone. I read his poetry hard, looking for an idea for a children's poem. I finally thought of a poem about the difference between the silent, secret self and the self that is seen by the outside world. Or, to put it more in children's language, the difference between the way you seem to be to others and the way you really are. When I gave this idea to my classes, I read aloud three short poems by Lawrence which stressed the silent, secret self: "Trees in the Garden," "Nothing to Save," and "The White Horse." "The White Horse," particularly, had a strong effect on some of the poems, such as this one by a girl in the sixth grade:

My Own Little World

We go to the beach
I look at the sea
My mother thinks I stare
My father thinks I want to go in the water.
But I have my own little world.
I stare,
I see myself
I walk along the beach
Not another soul
But me.
I walk to a white horse
Snowy is her name
I get on
I hold tight to her manes
I nudge her slightly
She walks
The sun is setting
The sea is quiet
The sand is moist
The air is tender
The sky is all the colors of the rainbows
I kick her harder
My hair blows in the wind
On to the destiny, of nothing
It seems endless
I think perhaps it is
My own little world.

Amy Levy, 6

This poem is especially like Lawrence's work in its emphasis on a separate world of the self. Other poems less like his in details owe partly to his influence, I think, their depth of feeling and their seriousness. A few weeks earlier I had read some of his poems ("Fish" and "The Snake") in conjunction with the Being An Animal Poem and they had had little effect. I realized then that Lawrence's way of talking to and about animals, though I remembered it as simple and conversational, actually incorporated adult attitudes which would make it somewhat remote from children—

> Fish, oh Fish,
> So little matters!
>
> Whether the waters rise and cover the earth . . .
>
> *D. H. Lawrence,* "Fish"

In talking about mysterious silence, however, Lawrence had a tone my students could use—

> They are so silent they are in another world . . .
>
> *D. H. Lawrence,* "The White Horse"

All this suggests the possibility of teaching literature in the schools in conjunction with writing. It might help children get more out of both. It was, in any case, in this way that D. H. Lawrence, by being incorporated into poems by Amy Levy and others, became part of the literary tradition of P.S. 61.

III Different Classes and Grades

There were differences in attitudes toward poetry and in the kind of poetry written by the different grades at the school. These differences were mainly due to age, though the personalities of the teachers and of the most influential students were also a factor. As poets, the primary graders tended to be buoyant and bouncy, the third graders wildly and crazily imaginative, the fourth graders warmly sensuous and lyrical, the fifth graders quietly sensuous and intellectual, and the sixth graders ironic (sometimes even slightly bitter), secretive, and emotional. These are generalizations, and I saw important variations from one year to another. Information more useful to a teacher may be that for an almost guaranteed warm and excited response to poetry the first time (as well as thereafter) I would recommend third and fourth graders. The great and terrible onset of self-consciousness seems to begin around the fifth grade, and if children haven't written before that they may at first be a bit diffident about it. By the sixth grade they are more so, and by then some students have already decided that poetry is not for them, and they are tough to convince that they're wrong (though it can be done). Primary graders are a pleasure, and they like writing too, but to get a solid body of work going it might be best to start with slightly older children. Only for the first few weeks. After that one should move in on everybody, since they will all, if one goes at it the right way, enjoy it a lot.

The way classes respond and how readily and how well they write has much to do also with how much poetry they have already written. This year's fifth graders, who have been writing poems on and off since third grade, turn out poems as naturally as an apple tree turns out blossoms. I don't mean that they're facile, but that they know what writing a poem is all about. If you asked them to skip, they would know how to do that too. Even with this class, however, I never find it sufficient merely to ask them to write a poem. If I want them to enjoy it, I look for an idea that will challenge them and teach them something new, and I do what I can to help them feel its pleasures and possibilities. For the most recent poem I gave them, the one using Spanish words, I found it good to have them do the kind of associations we had done for Color Poems and Noise Poems. I asked them to close their eyes and listen while I said "night" and then *"la noche."* I asked them what color each word was, and which was darker. (*La noche* turned out to be darker, and more purple.) I did the same for sky and *cielo,* and for star and *estrella.* This helped them, I think, to get a sensuous sense of the Spanish words as well as of the English ones and made them eager to use them in what they wrote.

> In invierno the sky is azul.
> And in verano the cielo is light blue . . .

> *Esther Garcia, 5*

Children of different ages responded to assignments differently. Primary graders wrote Wish Poems with the exuberance of those who think their wishes might come true; for the fourth graders there was a line, though it was blurry, between what was possible and what wasn't; many sixth graders could only regard wishing ironically—

> I wish J.V. would turn into a Ruffles Potato Chip . . .

> *Andrew Barish, 6*

On the other hand, sixth graders took the I Seem To Be / But Really I Am Poem very seriously: it was a subject a little more appropriate to their stage of life than wishing. The fourth graders found it mainly a subject for joking—

> I seem to be purple
> But really I am pink

> *Thomas Rogaski, 4*

Different suggestions about the poems are helpful to children of different ages. How does a dog go? What do you hear in bed at night? are good questions to help primary graders with their Noise Poems, but too young for ten-to-twelve-year-olds.

The way of teaching I have described worked as well with so-called deprived or disadvantaged children as it had with others. The children I worked with who had problems in reading and writing were those in "N.E." * classes at P.S. 61 and some of the students in the writing workshops at Muse. The reason I say "so-called" is because the words *deprived* and *disadvantaged* may be thought to apply to the children's imaginations and their power to create things, and they do not. The tragedy—and for a teacher, the hope and the opportunity—is not that these children lack imagination, but that it has been repressed and depressed, among other places at school, where their difficulties with writing and reading are sometimes a complete bar to their doing anything creative or interesting. They needn't be. Degree of literacy certainly makes a difference in a child's ability to write easily and confidently, but it does not form his imagination. The power to see the world in a strong, fresh and beautiful way is a possession of all children. And the desire to express that vision is a strong creative and educational force. If there is a barrier in its way—in this case it was writing—the teacher has to find a way to break that barrier down, or to circumvent it.

Since writing was the problem, I had them say their poems out loud. So that they would excite and inspire each other as much as possible, I had them compose their poems together.

---

* N.E. stands for "non-English speaking," a rather misleading administrative term. Children I taught in such classes could all speak English, and all except one or two "language learners" could write it, though often with some difficulty in grammar and spelling.

When we did these spoken collaboration poems, I would sit with from six to fifteen students around a table or in a circle of chairs. I would propose a theme, such as Wishes or Lies, and they would make up lines, which I would write down. When we thought we had enough, we stopped, and I read the poem back to them. Often in the course of composition I read it back too, to re-inspire the students and to show them where we were. I usually called on them in order, though occasionally I yielded to the irrepressible inspiration of someone who couldn't wait to tell me his line. I found writing—or even typing—better than using a tape recorder. The time it takes to write or type a line gives the children a chance to work a little more on their ideas. And when the work is read back, it sounds more like a poem because all the incidental noise (laughter, shouted comments) is left out.

These collaborations almost always made the children want to make up, and usually to write, poems of their own. Composing a poem together is inspiring: the timid are given courage by braver colleagues; and ideas too good to belong to any one child are transformed, elaborated on, and topped. Lies are particularly exciting in this regard, but Wishes, Comparisons, Noises, I used To/But Now, and some other themes can also become exhilaratingly competitive—

> I wish I was an apple
> I wish I was a steel apple
> I wish I was a steel apple so when people bit me their teeth
>   would fall out . . .

So a subject is built up, starting with something rather plain and becoming deeper and more interesting in its elaboration. The teacher can help this process along by interposing questions: Any special kind of apple? Why? Are there any other fruits anyone would like to be? Hands. Shouts. "I want to be an orange!" (spoken with an air of great discovery and a feeling of creative power). How big an orange? "I want to be an orange as big as the school!" More hands. "I wish school was a big orange and New York City was a fruit store and my block was a pineapple!" Excited by this atmosphere, and often having stored up ideas of their own which they are eager to express, children are willing to face even the uncertainties of writing.

It's understandable that children with reading and writing difficulties might be shy of being natural and spontaneous in school. Often what they say is "corrected" for what's wrong in it before what's good in it is acknowledged. That makes it not much fun to talk. To help them be poets, I did just the opposite. I immediately praised whatever it was that was imaginative or funny or anything in what they said, and let the mistakes fall where they would. If I didn't understand something I would ask, but I made it clear I wanted to know the exact word or meaning so I could get more out of the line. Once children sense a playful, encouraging, and esthetic (rather than corrective) attitude in the teacher, they become less shy and more willing to take risks.

The speed with which "non-writing" children can become excited about writing poetry was made very clear to me in working with Mrs. Magnani's fourth grade "N.E." class. Ron Padgett came with me the first time I visited this class, and he, Mrs. Magnani, and I each worked with about twelve students. We had decided to do a Lie Poem Collaboration. Lying, for all its bad points in daily living, is a very quick way to the world of the imagination. It is also a competitive pastime. Like the Mississippi riverboat men in *Huckleberry Finn*, the children at P.S. 61 were eager to do each other one better, to tell an even bigger, more astonishing untruth: I live on the moon; I live half the year on the moon and half on the sun; I live on all the planets: January on Jupiter, March on Mars, December on the Planet of the Apes. Different kinds of lies could also please and astonish: I am ten years older than my teacher; I like school. These fourth graders, with just the slightest encouragement from us, began to create strange realities with great gusto. When we read the group poems back to them, they were very excited. At all three tables they demanded to write Lie Poems of their own.

Once the students began to write down their individual poems, there was terrible chaos, since they were bursting with untruthful inspiration, eager to write, and unable to spell half the words they wanted to use. All the time they were writing, there would be a few students, frantically excited, shouting at me at the head of the table. I couldn't tell them, as I had told children in other classes (and even there not always with success), just to write the word any way they could, that spelling didn't matter, I would understand it anyway. They knew perfectly well they couldn't write it at all, and I knew I wouldn't be able to tell January from an elephant if I didn't show them how the words were spelled. Showing turned out to be better than telling. I had paper in front of me, and when they asked me a word, I wrote it down—rather, I printed it—as fast as I could. Telling them how to spell all the words would have taken forever, since no one could hear anything I said. It is tiring to work at the center of an inspired mob, and also rather heady. The noise and the activity had other values for the children: they were part of an excitement which enabled them to forget their "illiteracy" long enough to write poetry.

Another cause of the high spirits of this class was my asking them to put some of their lies in Spanish. I thought their knowledge of a second language was clearly an advantage, and I wanted them to know it. They liked using Spanish, and they also enjoyed translating for me when I didn't know what they had written. The mere fact that a word or phrase was in Spanish made it interesting and amusing to them. They all spoke English, but English was the language of school, whereas Spanish was a kind of secret. Very few could write Spanish, in fact, so those who could helped the others to spell Spanish words as I was helping everyone to spell English ones.

After this beginning in which the children had spoken and written Lie Poems they were excited about poetry, and though spelling problems remained they went on liking to write it. They wrote a good deal. Like everyone else's poetry, theirs became richer and freer as a result of the poems they listened to and those they wrote themselves—

> In spring I play
> I eat in spring
> I do my work in spring
> I'm good in spring
> I'm doing my things in spring
> Spring, Spring, you're mine
> Spring is the color of a rose
> If I was spring
> Spring, Spring I'm calling you
> Spring, Spring play with me
> Spring, Spring I love you.
>
> *Maria Mesen, 4*

> The third eye can see inside me
> The third eye can see the hosts
> The third eye can see Puerto Rico
> The third eye can see my voice
> The third eye can see my bones
> The third eye can see the wind . . .
>
> *Robert Melendez, 4*

As in groups of good readers and writers, some children with writing problems are more inclined toward poetry than others; and some who can hardly write are more imaginative poets than many who write without mistakes. What seemed most important was that, of the children I taught, every one had the capacity to write poetry well enough to enjoy it himself and usually well enough to give pleasure to others, whether it was entire poems or surprising and beautiful images, lines, or combinations of words.

The educational advantages of a creative intellectual and emotional activity which children enjoy are clear. Writing poetry makes children feel happy, capable, and creative. It makes them feel more open to understanding and appreciating what others have written (literature). It even makes them want to know how to spell and say things correctly (grammar). Once Mrs. Magnani's students were excited about words, they were dying to know how to spell them. Learning becomes part of an activity they enjoy—when my fifth graders were writing their Poems Using Spanish Words they were eager to know more words than I had written on the board; one girl left the room to borrow a dictionary. Of all these advantages, the main one is how writing poetry makes children feel: creative; original; responsive, yet in command.

IV   Poetry in the Schools

Since children like writing poetry, and since it's such a good thing for them in so many ways, what can be done in the schools to help them write it? One thing is for a poet from outside to come and teach in the schools as I did. Another is for teachers already there to try teaching poetry. At P.S. 61 there was a great change. A lot of children there are writing poetry now who would not have been otherwise, and their feelings about it are different too. They may have had a distant respect for poetry before, but now it belongs to them. They really like it. Some have written twenty or thirty poems and are still raring to go. It is not our mysterious charm for which Ron Padgett and I are wildly applauded when we go into the fifth grade classroom and for which shrieks of joy have greeted us in other classrooms too. It is the subject we bring, and along with that, our enthusiasm for what the students do with it. It occurred to me some time ago that I was as popular and beloved a figure at P.S. 61 as certain art and music teachers had been at my grade school in Cincinnati. And that I was doing more or less what they had done, though in a form of art that, for all its prestige, has been relatively ignored in the schools.

The change in the children is the most evident, but the teachers have changed too. Once they saw what the children were doing, they became interested themselves. They have given their own poetry writing assignments, they put children's poems on bulletin boards along with their artwork, and they have the children read their poems in class and in school assembly. Before, I think, poetry was kind of a dead subject at the school (dormant, anyway). For all their good will, the teachers didn't see a way to connect it with the noisy, small, and apparently prosy creatures they faced in the classroom. But now they have seen the connection, which is that children have a great talent for writing poetry and love to do it.

New York City   KENNETH KOCH
January 1970

Class Collaborations

Third Grade

Poem

I wish I were with Charlie Brown in a blue shirt in France
I wish that I would wear a Popeye hat the color of the hat will
    be white Popeye is in the country
I wish I was in red Israel with Little Abner
I wish I was red with Mighter in Japan
I wish I was in Jordan right in the garden I wish it was blue
    I wish I was a Queen
I wish I was green with Superman in Negev Desert
I wish that I was with Little Orphan Annie in W. D. C. in
    my light blue shirt
I wish that I was in New York
I wish I were the color red I would be Thor and I would be in
    the Unpt
I wish I was Blondie in the color sea green and the state of
    California
I wish that I was Popeye with a yellow dress on me and in
    South Carolina

I wish I can see Superman in person I wish I love the color
    blue which Superman wears
I wish I was Olive Oyl in Popeye in California and I am
    white
I wish that I could be wearing a purple dress in California
    with Popeye
I wish Charlie Brown is blue in the United States
I wish I lived in Brooklyn with Popeye in his new hat
I wish that I was in France with Popeye with the color red
I wish I had a color gray with the state of Asia with the name
    of Popeye
I wish I was yellow with Popeye in Pennsylvania
I wish I was yellow and I would come from the country I wish
    I was Popeye
I wish I had a horse with blue eyes I would name him Porky
    Pig we would live in Kentucky
I wish I was with Popeye in Paris with a red color on my face
I wish I was red and Popeye in Europe state
I wish I could be with Top Cat with Blue New York in a
    place called ace-play
I wish I was Charlie Brown in blue Saudi Arabia

Mrs. Schapiro's class

Fourth Grade

I wish there was a Blondie who would be in a brown
  Australia
I wish there was a Charlie Brown, yellow, fickle feather,
  France
I wish I was Snoopy fighting the Red Baron in Germany
I wish I was with Charlie Brown in blue Chincoteague
I wish my brother and I would stop fighting red in New York
I wish I worked with Charlie Brown and his gang
I wish Orphan Annie didn't have big ball eyes
I wish I were Violet in England
I wish I was in Mexico I wish I love the color pink I wish I
  was in China
I wish Bugs Bunny hadn't put the white car from New York
  in the bathroom
I wish Bugs Bunny didn't climb the blue tree in Turkey
  Land
I wish I were with Encyclopedia Brown crossing the blue
  Atlantic Ocean to Germany
I wish Spiderman wasn't with purple Pennsylvania
I wish I was Blondie and dressed in blue in Turkey
I wish I was Little Orphan Annie with a bright red dress in
  France
I wish I would be with Flash on a green board in New York
  City
I wish I could be James Bond in the movie I wish my suit
  could be the color blue I wish I lived in Asia and in
  Africa
I wish I had a puppy and he was very cute and he was brown
  and a little white. He lived in the country.

I wish Flash wasn't so red to go so fast in Central City
I wish I was with Lady in Texas and with all the clowns

Mrs. Wiener's class

Fifth and Sixth Grades

Feelings at P.S. 61

I wish that Charlie Brown would go to Japan.

I wish that the sky was blue over New York while Dick Tracy chased a yellow car.

I wish Charlie Brown would go to London.

I wish that I was Dick Tracy in a black suit in England.

I wish that I were a Supergirl with a red cape; the city of Mexico will be where I will live.

I wish that I were Veronica in South America. I wish that I could see the blue sky.

I wish that I were a blue robin. I would fly to Mexico and Canada and visit Donald Duck.

I wish that I were Lucy so I could get a red dress and go to London.

I wish that I were Charlie Brown eating a burnt, brown, greasy turkey with china on the table.

I wish that Louie would go to Purple Polkadotland.

I wish I were a flash, fast as Flash. I would be wearing the color red and the color yellow just like the sun. I would walk across New York.

I wish Charlie Brown were in New York City with his big white dog Snoopy.

I wish that Lucy and Charlie Brown would go to London.

I wish that Snoopy was in Mexico City wearing a red, blue, and yellow crazy suit.

I wish that Spiderman would make a blue web over New York.

I wish that I were red-haired Orphan Annie, who lived in Sweden.

I wish that Lucy would turn red and go to Germany.

I wish I could be Charlie Brown in China.

I wish that I were Dondi in Africa, with a purple machine gun.

I wish that Dick Tracy was in Red China.

I wish Dick Tracy would go to Maine so his black tie wouldn't be so plain.

I wish that Charley Chan would come to Washington to see the fields of olive green and meet my friend Cecil McDean.

I wish I were Brenda Starr and went to yellow India.

I wish that when Superman flies over New York he would turn green with envy.

I wish that blue New York was where Dick Tracy lived.

I wish that New York was all blue and had Mighty Mouse as our Mayor.

I wish that blue Little Abner lived in Japan.

I wish I had Snoopy and he owned me. I wish I had a green canary that was born in Brazil. Yes, it would be fun.

Mrs. Weick's and Mr. Bowman's classes

Fifth Grade

Goodbye, Mr. Koch

Be sure to go to the German Alps and say hello to my Dad
Eat a lot of apple strudel in Germany
Maybe you can dig a tunnel and find another tunnel where
    prisoners are escaping from East Berlin
Eat all the Italian type spaghetti
Try making some pizza
Eat matzoh balls
Knock down the Leaning Tower of Pisa
And you'll have a lot of help: it'll be leaning already
Go to Naples and drink wine
And visit Sibernus for me
You can roam around Rome
Feed somebody to the lions at the Coliseum
Or go chariot racing
Eat the bottom ring of the ice cream in Naples
Be the third Columbus
Take some Spanish dancing lessons
See the bullfights in Madrid
But don't faint
When they pick you to be the matador too
Run a million miles away
Don't eat any enchiladas
They're too hot
Don't forget your bathing suit
Make sure you don't drown
We want you back
Don't go crazy with your language
Don't forget to button up your overcoat

Send us a couple of cheeses from Switzerland
Don't break your leg skiing
Send me a sample of snow
In a hot stove
Don't go on any Israeli Airlines
Don't meet the Wolfman
Don't work in the Radium Dial Company
You'll get leukemia
Mrs B. works there—they call her that—she had leukemia
Make your hair grow long and join the Beatles or buy a wig
Hold your ears at 12 o'clock when you're near Big Ben
Don't watch the girls in miniskirts (this is a recording)
Bring an umbrella and bring an overcoat
Go see Queen Elizabeth and bring back some of her jewels
Bring Charlie Chaplin with you
Install windshield wipers on your eyeglasses
Visit Camelot and steal King Arthur's crown
And meet the stupid Knight in Red
And marry Guinevere
Don't run into a bobby
Go on top of the Tower and don't fall off
England swings like a pendulum do
With the crown and jewels buy an airplane
Get some feathers and make them into wings and fly back
Walk back so you won't get highjacked
Swim the English Channel and fly back
Go by boat and take some seasick pills
(Don't forget to take Guinevere)
Don't forget to write

Mrs. Weick's class

Class Collaborations

The first three poems in this section are the first written by third graders, fourth graders, and a combined class of fifth and sixth graders. "Goodbye, Mr. Koch" was written much later.

For the first three poems each student wrote one line on a sheet of paper. There were rules: every line had to begin with "I wish" and had to include a color, a comic-strip character, and a city or country. Many other good combinations are possible: any elements that will excite a child's imagination and test his ingenuity: animals, months, makes of automobile, planets, things to drink, birds, states. The children are likely to have good suggestions. After the lines were passed in, I read them aloud as a poem. It was a good first assignment; it made the children excited about writing poetry.

"Goodbye, Mr. Koch" was an oral class collaboration which Ron Padgett elicited from the fifth graders after I had left the school to go to Europe last year. He asked them to mention various places in Europe and what they wanted me to do in them. In oral collaborations by the whole class, one can ask for lines in a certain order or call on children who raise their hands. I found that certain children tend to dominate this kind of composition; they are hard to resist because their ideas are usually so good, but I always tried to get lines from as many students as possible. The most eager ones can be relied on when the poem gets bogged down.

Group poems are an excellent way to get children excited about poetry, to help them overcome their inhibitions about it, and in general to inspire them to write it. I found spoken collaborations especially useful with children with problems in writing. Collaborations are also effective in reviving a class's interest in poetry, if it is flagging. Collaborative poems dealt with in other parts of this book are Sestinas and Collaborations by Two Students.

Collaborative poems are an old literary tradition. Linked verse was the major form of Japanese poetry for centuries. Poets wrote together in ancient China and in medieval Provence. Wordsworth and Coleridge tried to write *The Ancient Mariner* together, but Wordsworth stopped. The surrealists are the best-known modern practitioners of this kind of writing. It can be done in a great many ways, of which I had the children try only a few.

Wishes

Primary Grade

I wish my rabbit would not lick me!
I wish that I can eat in a tree like dinner.
I wish I could eat chicken all night long!
I wish that I was a giraffe because they got a long neck!
I wish I could go to the river and eat meat!
I wish I was a monkey to eat banana! I wish I was as bad as
    my brother!

Chip Wareing

I wish me and my brother and my friend Paul were birds.
I wish the world and school were candy.
I wish we could eat gum in class.
I wish we could break glass.
I wish I was the best reader in the whole world.

David Jeanpierre

I wish I was a little grandmother
I wish I were a bird to fly
I wish I were a teacher to teach
I wish I were a little doll
I wish I were a dog to bark
I wish I were a Girl Scout
I wish I were a nurse to help sick people
I wish I were going to the moon
I wish I were a cat
I wish I were policewoman

Diana Maza

I wish that the streets were ice to make it nice.
I wish we lived under water.
I wish we had $1.00 dollars.
I wish that we lived on the sun.

Berton Salib

I wish I had a diamond
I wish I had a bike
I wish I had a cat
I wish I had a puppy
I wish I had a friend.

Richard Ulloa

I wish I was Dodo.
I wish I was a bird so I could fly in the sky.
I wish I was a lion so I could roar all the time. I wish I was
a dog so I could bark all the time.
I wish I was a doll so they could carry me all the time.
I wish I was soso, and I wish I was bobo too. I wish I was a
book so the children could read me.

Zaida Rivera

I wish I was an actress
I wish there were no boys
I wish there were only girls
I wish the street was ice cream

Leda Mesen

I wish I could go swimming
I wish I could go to the store
I wish I could go to the store
I wish I could go in the air.

Rosemary Cole

Third Grade

I wish I had a white horse.
I wish I had a parrot that could sing.
I wish I had a horse farm.
I wish I could do my homework in one second.
I wish I had 100 comic books.
I wish I had 12,000 crayons.
I wish I had the whole series of Bobbsey Twins books.
I wish that I still lived in Texas.
I wish I had 1,000 horses.

Eliza Bailey

I Wish

I wish I was a strawberry
I wish I could be in a book
I wish they sold houses for nothing
I wish I could become small as big as a pencil
I wish I had a lot of clothes that didn't cost anything
I wish I could do my homework without a pencil and do my
    homework without writing anything.

Ilona Baburka

I wish I was a hippie to wear fancy stuff
I wish I had a certain teacher like the one I had
I wish I had a million dogs to kill one each night

Richard Ulloa

I wish in the summer it snowed like
ice cream and every day
I would take a cup and
fill it with ice cream
instead of going to a Carvel
and if it really snowed hard
I would make a snow man with the ice cream
and when it would stop snowing
I would eat the ice cream snow man.

Lynne Reiff

I wish I were a key
I wish the boys were pigs
I wish I were the Three Stooges
I wish I were Green Acres.

Rosemary Cole

I Wish

I wish I had a home of my own.
I wish I had a baby brother.
I wish I had a dog.
I wish I had long hair.
I wish I had a cat.
I wish I had a baby sister
I wish I was a cat.
I wish I was a dog.
I wish I was a tiger.
I wish I was a lion.
I wish I was a looking glass.
I wish I were the sun and the moon.

Marion Mackles

I Wish I Had

I wish I was a millionaire
I wish I had a baby chair
I wish I was a baby
The smallest in the world
I wish I was the smartest person in the world
I wish I had a money tree
And I wish I was a man.

Michael Freihofer

I wish I owned a jet. I would fly to Hawaii and Miami and I would have the stewardess give me some steak and brownies and cake and cookies and ice cream soda, the soda I would want would be Coke, 7-up, Pepsi, gingerale. I would give my friends rides to school and give people free rides to all different places like Japan, China, Hollywood, and Spain. I would bring food to the Biafran children.

Andrew Norden

I Wish

I wish that I was the richest man in the world
I wish that I had a big big boat
I wish that I was the tallest person in the world
And I wish that I lived in the country and I had a horse

I wish that I could change into anyone I want
I wish that there were only three people in the world
That are me, Michael and Billy
I wish that people had ten eyes so that you could see
  everywhere
I wish that people could live for 1000 years

Author unknown

I wish I was a chocolate-covered flying horse.
I wish the boys were pigs except my brother.
I wish I was a bird so I can tell the birds Be quiet.

Marie Flanagan

I wish I was an airplane so I could look at the sky. I would throw everyone out of my airplane so I could be alone.

Melissa Blitz

I wish I was a painter and when someone looks out of their window I would paint their face. If I was Irish I would paint a firehouse green. I would paint Jackie Gleason red. I would paint myself black.

Steven Lenik

I wish I was a cough drop. I'd go down someone's throat and tell the cough to get out of *here!* Coughs don't belong in here!

Berton Salib

Fourth Grade

I wish I had a pony with a tail like hair
I wish I had a boyfriend with blue eyes and black hair I
    would be so glad
I wish I was Sleeping Beauty so I would go to sleep and they
    would come and kiss me
I wish I had a daughter with blond hair and light green eyes
I wish I could be the biggest dancer in the world
I wish I had every miniskirt my sister has

Milagros Diaz

Ballet

I wish I could do fantastic steps like 51 pirouettes in one
    minute.
I wish I could be very famous.
I wish I could leap high into the air and land softly on my
    toes.
I wish I could dance in every country in the world.
I wish I could become a ballet dancer.
My biggest wish is that all of these wishes would come true.

Melanie Popkin

Spring Fever

Spring is here. I can
Feel it in my bones. I wish
I had some thing that
Would prove my bones are
Correct. But what about
The trees? The trees
Prove my bones are
Correct. Why they're all
Green like the wonderful
Bright green rye grass
By the end of the walk
The daffodils at the end
Of the road. And I feel
So lazy because of my
Spring fever.

> *Jean Morrison*

I wish I had a puppy
I wish I had a chimpanzee
I wish I was a Supergirl
I wish I had a kitten to do my homework
And a chimpanzee to do my housework

> *Ruby Johnson*

I wish I was a bird so I would knock on people's heads. I wish I was a monkey so I would eat bananas. I wish I was an elephant so when I walk everything would shake. I wish I had a gorilla for a mother so I would eat bananas. I wish I was rich, I would have the animals in the houses and the people in the forest. I wish I was a mouse so I would scare people.

Anthony Hernandez

Oh! If I had a wish I'd want, I'd say, I'd like to have all my
    wishes come true.
I'd wish I had a mink coat.
I'd wish I could be a movie star.
I'd wish to live in England.
I'd wish for peace in the world.
I'd wish for diamonds
(A girl's best friend).
I'd wish to be rich.
I'd wish to have Mrs. Wiener through Elementary School,
    Junior High School, and College.
I'd wish to only say "Ah" and my brother would be nice to
    me.
I'd wish to get 100% on all my tests.

Annie Clayton

I wish I was a bird to fly overhead.
I wish I was a duck to swim in a pond.
I wish I was a wild horse to run free.
I wish I was a pig to jump in the mud.
I wish I was a cow to moo all day long.
I just wish I was an animal.

Lenora Calanni

I wish that school would not exist
And it would ride away in a car.
Keeping itself to Heaven—no
I think it deserved punishment
But it is no use dreaming now
Of school does not exist
And keeping itself away in a car
Out of the way of us.
And then I wish summer wouldn't end.
No matter what or why
And it would stay with us all year.
Oh, wouldn't that be nice?
But we have no control over seasons
So we'll have to wish and dream
That the Lord will grant our wish
Of summer all year long!

Lisa Jill Braun

I Wish I Could Fly

I wish I could fly
And fly all over town
I would go through houses and pay a visit to everyone
I would go to Charles C's house to talk and have some fun
And then I would fly home to have fun the rest of the day
At my own little house

Martin Freihofer

Sometimes I wish I had my own kitten.
Sometimes I wish I owned a puppy.
Sometimes I wish we had a color T.V.
Sometimes I wish for a room of my own.
And I wish all my sisters would disappear.
And I wish we would live in the country.
And I wish we didn't have to go to school.
And I wish my little sister would find her nightgown.
And I wish even if she didn't she wouldn't wear mine.

Erin Harold

A Couple of Wishes

If I had a chance to be granted a wish I'd wish to be smarter
    than anyone in my class.
To be able to know math or science or any subject questions
    on the spot.
I wish I could be the greatest scientist on earth.
To be able to solve problems or invent a new vaccine to cure
    a sickness.
I'd be famous and great. The most famous person in the
    world.

Argentina Wilkinson

If I was a bird I'd wish that I could fly.
If I was a cow I'd wish that I could moo 100 times.
If I was a dog I'd wish that I could bow wow.
If I was a table I would like it.
If I was a ring Zulma would like me.
If I was a doll Marilyn would like me.
If I was a little girl I'd wish that I had a doll.
If I was a little fish Zulma would not like me.
If I was a cat I'd wish to play with a dog.

Mildred Camacho

I wish I was still a baby
I wish I was the smartest boy
I wish I was a street so that cars would run over me
I wish I had a million dollars
I wish I had a car
I wish I had a ten-speed bike
I wish I lived in Puerto Rico
I want to ride my car there
I wish I was a traffic cop.

Frank Colletti

I wish I was a lion with my brother.
I wish I meet the monkey.
I wish I was 8th Man and Flash too.
I wish I was the strongest boy in the world.
I wish I had 1000 dollars.
I wish a turtle gave me a ride.
I wish me my brother and my mother and my father were
    rich.
I wish there were no girls only me and my mother father and
    my brother AND
That's the end of the story.

Jesus Perez

I wish I was a country so they would like me. I wish I was a
sea so fishes would live in me.

I wish the world was candy.

I wish we would play in school all day.

I wish we would have no school.

I wish we had no homework.

I wish we had everything in the store free.

I wish we had *no* shoes.

I wish we had no hair so you wouldn't mess around with it
all day.

I wish I could see through everything.

I wish I was Supergirl.

I wish I was Superman's girlfriend.

I wish I was the moon.

I wish I was Mrs. Nobody.

I wish I was Mrs. Popeye the Sailor Girl with Popeye the
Sailor Man. I wish all the food was candy. I wish I was
invisible.

I wish I was one year old so I wouldn't go to school.

I wish I could fly.

I wish I was magic so if I wanted to go to Japan I wouldn't
have to go by plane.

I wish my puppy was Superdog. I wish I was a star twinkling
in the sky.

I wish I was rich.

I wish I was the best singer in the world. I wish I was a plum
so they could eat me and see what their stomach looks
like. I wish I was a mirror so I could look at everybody.
I wish I was my mother's fairy so if she wanted something
I would be able to give it to her.

Mayra Morales

I Wish

I wish I was a Super human being.
I wish I could see what happened long ago in the past.
I wish I could go anywhere I want to.
I wish I was a genius.
I wish the snow was one yard high.
I wish I had my own puppy dog.
I wish I had my own tree that grew oranges.
I wish I saw what the moon looks and really feels like.
I wish I could make it snow, rain, and make it sunny.
I wish I could do everything in the world.

Ilona Baburka

Fifth Grade

Wishy Washy Wishes

I wish Amy would stop wearing miniskirts and stop acting
    like Twiggy.
I wish I could go to California and go surfing.
I wish I had a motor boat.
I wish that it would be against the law to have teachers talk.
I wish I could have anything I wanted.
I wish my bedroom would stop shrieking.
I wish my friends wouldn't show off so much.
I wish my cat would be a singer in Lincoln Center.
I wish a boy in my class would jump in the Hudson River.

Debbie Novitsky

Why does the American flag have to be red white and blue?
I wish the stripes were yellow and white, the stars blue and
    green and of course blue-green.
Why does China have to be named China? It sounds like
    some dishes being in a sink getting washed.
Why do the Hawaiian trees have grass skirts?
I wish they'd be regular trees and stop showing off.
I think this world is upside down I wish this world was down-
    side up.

Gloria Peters

Sixth Grade

If I ruled the world, I would stop
all poverty by ridding the world of money.
I'd save the world of violence
by ridding it of guns.
And to every man ten beautiful girls.
So people can't steal
I'd give everyone seven
of the best cars in the world.
And this way our world
will be the right way.

Roberto Marcilla

I wish that I could own a plane
And fly it all around
Swerving, turning different ways
Knocking other planes down.

I'd shoot down buildings
Scaring people through
The Air Force is after me
They don't know the things I'd do

I'd fly around the world
And into the sun
It could never happen
But it would be fun.

Jonathan Spaet

I Wish

I wish I was a beautiful chick who could be in any period of
    life
In the future in the past would be nice
Being Cleopatra in Egypt with handsome men at my feet
How about Annie Oakley putting on a show
Or being a pirate enjoying the gold
Even the first woman president in 3002
Also a bloodthirsty vampire scaring the men
Or Einstein inventing a potion for invisible guys
Maybe the first to live in an alligator plane in 2026

Emilia Scifo

I wish I could find a chest full of money
Nice crisp green money
Lots of it
In 10's and 20's
I wish I could get revenge on L.B. for putting me on a com-
    mittee to do a report on Ancient India
I wish J.V. would turn into a Ruffles Potato Chip
I wish that I found the world's largest diamond and there
    were no Internal Revenue men to take all that nice green
    money for taxes
I wish D.C. would start using mouthwash
I wish that Paul's wish which is "I wish Pug will disappear"
    will come true.

Andrew Barish

Wishes

Wishes make a very good early writing assignment. Children are great makers of wishes, and they love to write about them. Asking them to do so gives them a whole lot of new subject matter they usually don't think about in school. To help them with form I suggested that they begin every line with "I wish," and to make them feel free about what they said I suggested that they make their wishes as wild and crazy as they liked.

In my primary class I asked the children to write one-line Wish Poems to begin with. They were excited when I read these back to them, and afterwards they wrote longer ones. One-line poems can be good preparation for other themes, too.

Wishes are one of the best themes for spoken collaborative poems in classes where the children have difficulty writing. Like lies, they engage children's imaginations quickly and get them interested in making up poetry.

Comparisons

Primary Grade

A butterfly is like a colorful flying rainbow.
Clouds are like flying ice cream.
Cotton is like and looks like clouds, that are as soft as pillows.
A big green lollipop is like a green apple.
Hair is like spaghetti.
School is like a rotten house.
An orange is like a pink flower.
A pig is like a girl.

Oscar Marcilla

Pencil sharpenings are like snow.
A witch's coat is like a mussel shell.
The sun is as red as a fire.
The earth is like a giant ball.

Berton Salib

A fat balloon is like a pickle.
A moon is like an egg.
The air is like an orange.
Snow is like vanilla ice cream.
When paper is flying it is like a flying ice cream cone.

Melissa Blitz

A toothpick is like my brother.
A moon is like a banana.
A plane is like a bird.
A pear is like a light.

Lynne Reiff

My shirt is as blue as the sky
My hair is as black as my shoes
My pants are as green as a leaf
My sweater is as white as the snow

Richard Ulloa

A flag is like a balloon flying in the sky
A ball is like a wheel rolling down the street
A piece of paper is like snow falling down

Valerie Chassé

Thunder is like bowling
Clouds are like a feather
The sun is like a yellow balloon in the sky
A tiger is like the beating of drums.

Robert Mattei

A red big ball is like a circle
A big ball is like a ball
A blue big bat is like a stick
A big green hat is like a ball
A yellow ball is like a hat
A big red hat is like a circle.

Jennie Ortiz

A dog is like a bushy piece of cotton. The flag is like lots of
   colors. The sky is blue.
A girl is soft.
A boy is like a rock.
The sun is like a yellow balloon.

Myrna Diaz

Third Grade

Comparison Poem

My hair is as silky as the wind
My eyes are as green as the sea
A clock is as white as snow
Red is as colorful as my cheeks
The flag is as striped as a shirt
My skin is as red as a white rose
I am as bad as my good brother
I am as hairy as my bald father
The flag is as red, white, and blue as the sun's reflection
I am as big as an ant
I am as big as a pencil
I am as free as the wind
My hand is as big as the sky
I am as red as a fly
I am as black as a black rose
I am as funny as a funny
I am as bright as the moon
I will be as smart as a butterfly
I am as good as a burglar
I am as great as a mouse
I am as bored as a party
My turtle is as pretty as me
I am as pretty as a purple rose
I am as pretty as a garden
My shirt is as green as grass

Marion Mackles

Fourth Grade

I Think

I think the snow is as white as vanilla custard.
I think that the rainbow is as colorful as a peacock's feathers.
I think the grass is as green as a ten-dollar bill.
I think perfume smells as sweet as a rose.
I think a bumpy mattress is just like a camel's back.
I think a deer is as graceful as a ballerina.

Melanie Popkin

The sky is as blue as the sea.
Our desks are as brown as our skin.
The sun is as bright as the light.
This room is as green as the grass.
Our teeth are as white as snow. Are your teeth as white as
    snow?
Yellow is the brightness of the sun.

Carmen Velez

Snow is as white as the sun shines.
The sky is as blue as a waterfall.
A rose is as red as a beating of drums.
The clouds are as white as the busting of a firecracker.
A tree is as green as a roaring lion.

Mary Minns

A cat's paw touching grass sounds like a cloud floating
A person's whisper is like a soft pillow.
Black ink is dark as midnight.

Lisa Jill Braun

The grass is as light as the sun.
The light is as bright as the sky.
The tree is as black as a bird.

Elizabeth Cabán

Winter Time

Snow is as white as a page.
Trees are as brown as a stage.
Roses are as pink as a book.
Teachers are as kind as a kitten.
Grass is as green as a couch.
Sleep is as furry as a kitten.
Flowers are as pretty as Mrs. Wiener.
Blue is as blue as a blue berry.

Theamondo Zaharias

The light is as bright as the sun.
The firelight burning is as bright as the hot sun.
The leaf of the grass is as bright as a ten-dollar bill.
The snow is as bright as a nightgown.
A rose is as colorful as an apple.
The moon is as black as a black apple burning.
A black pencil is as black as a black crayon.
A cat is as nice as mice.
School is the same as a home.
To play is to cry.

Maria Teresa Rivera

Scipullfinks

A plum in May is like a waterfall in June
A grape is like an olive but it's purple and blue
A pumpkin is a watermelon that is mentionable
But that's different with a scipullfink
Because it's unmentionable

Charles Conroy

The snow is as white as cotton. Is the sky as white as the
    clouds? Is the color yellow as the sun?
The deck is as brown as our skin.
My eyes are as brown as the wood.
And the sheep is as white as the paper.

Ruby Johnson

Snowflakes are like shining diamonds
A breeze is like the sky is coming to you
The sun is like golden bright earrings

Iris Torres

The Things Upstairs

The sky is as blue as a waterfall
The clouds are as white as marshmallows
The thunder is as loud as a beating drum
The rain is as cold as ice cubes
The lightning is as white as a pale face

Martin Freihofer

The red blood was as red as a red crayon.
The skin was as soft as a reindeer.
The clouds looked like snow falling down.
The wind looked like a bird flying in the air.
The tap looked like a woodpecker pecking.

Joseph Desberg

Anyway

The sky is as blue as thunder, but
The cat is as striped as an airplane take-off
The globe is as round as the wind

Tara Housman

Fifth Grade

My red mittens remind me of my goldfish
My sister's hair is as yellow as the sun
The lion roars like the wind
Her teeth were as white as the snow
My dress is as pink as my father's wine
The tap tap tap reminds me of my dog Tippytoes
The snow is like a feather falling from the sky.

Kathy Kennedy

My little green plant was like a big jungle
Her earrings were as green as a jade
When I opened the box I saw all the colors of the rainbow.
I saw reds as red as a book,
I saw greens as green as the sea on a calm, sunny day,
I saw yellows as yellow as a golden date tree in the fall.
I saw browns as brown as a little squirrel running up a tree.

Ruben Marcilla

The waves in the ocean are curl-free
A classroom is like a cage
Bad weather is gloomy like our school paint
Wooden desks are like woodchucks
The snow was like tar
The flower is a grounded bird
The bees are like teachers
The girl was as pink as roses
The cat sang like Judy Garland
A heart jumps up and down like a Superball.

Debbie Novitsky

Little brothers are like a group of drummers
Coats are like a sun in the summer
Trees on streets are like bear people
Leaves on trees are like pans
Heads are like haired baseballs
Fingers are like wiggly worms
Glasses are like eyes without eyeballs
Arms are like barks of trees.

Angel Torres

What's Like What?

My hair is like brown thread
But my cat's hair is like silver needles
   Black is as black as a drum thumping
But red is as red as a firecracker cracking
   Blue is as blue as an airplane flying
But green is as green as something growing
   The lamp is as silver as silver skyscrapers
But bells who are pink are pink as clinks and clinks
   Purple is as purple as a sock in the nose
But white is as white as screaming out
   The rain is as pink as pink tears
But orange is as orange as a blunk
   That's What's Like What!

Gloria Peters

The horses made a sound like a falling tree
The bird's song was like a tinkling bell
He turned as pale as the moon
The train shrieked like a woman screaming
The snow glistened like a rainbow
The cat's meow was like a baby crying.

Robin Harold

My dress is as pink as a rose
The color red is like blood
The zoo is like Africa
The light is as bright as a star
Cecilia's socks are as bright as a sun shining.

Magaly Rotgers

A rose is as rosy as Magaly's dress
The dog is as soft as a baby's hair
The sky is like a floating wave
The desk is as yellow as the desert
His hair is like a cool breeze
The baby is as soft as a feather.

Cecilia Kingwood

Comparison

Her blue eyes are like my stone in my ring
The red piece of paper is dark as my blood
Her pigtails look like a puppy's ears

Chalk is like a bright silver stone
Her golden hair looked like a golden bright sun
Her dark green eyes look like grass

The cat with the stripes looked like a tiger and zebra

His hair was as dark as the black cat
The glass looked like a shiny diamond
The yellow flower looked like a yellow bright dress

The smoke looked like his fluffy hair
The star looked like a big huge diamond.

Evelyn Rodriguez

The roses are as pink as the sun
The school is as pink as a rose
The flag is like a flying carpet in the breeze
The blackboard is as dark as the inside of a cave
The rainbow was like a giant candy cane
The pencil sharpener is like a baby chicken hatching out of
    an egg.

Hiran Rosario

Things That Look or Sound Like Something Else

His voice sounded like a stringed instrument.
Her hair was like a summer breeze.
The eraser was like a scuff of shoes.
Her face was as red as a ruby.
His ears were as pink as her lipstick.
The night was as black as ebony.
Her tan looked like sand.
Her sunburn was as red as paint.
His hair was as wavy as the ocean.
His veins were as green as grass.
The chalk was as white as a ghost.
His shirt was as orange as the sunset.

Ana Gomes

Microscopics Are Big

An ant is the beginning of a new universe
A needle leads a thread to the new universe
The needle is the locomotive and the thread is the train
The new world is black as a dungeon
The new world is a fairyland but in reality it is a thought.

Joel London

Sixth Grade

Venice reminds me of a model of an ant hill.

The eraser is like a dusty old book.

A glass reminds me of the Atlantic Ocean.

Roberto Marcilla

Under the sea is like Times Square.

A stubborn mule is like a dead battery.

Emilia Scifo

An octopus looks like a table and chair.

Helenann Crippen

Doing my poem in school reminds me of a grape ice.

Julie Malick

The inside of my desk looks like my block.

Ivette Garcia

A piece of chalk is like an ice cream soda.

Brian Blitz

The letter Z is like a moon, almost gone.

Ruth Cobrinik

Comparisons

Comparisons are something children enjoy, and they are a natural and important part of poetry. Children are very good at them once they feel they are free to say whatever comes into their minds. Their perceptions haven't been as conditioned as ours have by the sensible and the conventional, and if the sky looks like a white mouse they are capable of seeing it and, if they feel uninhibited, saying it. Anyone who has talked much to children knows this. So in encouraging them to feel free to make unusual comparisons I felt I wasn't urging them to be surrealistic, but to be themselves.

I held up a piece of chalk, a sheet of paper, a notebook, and asked them to compare each to something which was like it only in one way and not in others: the chalk is like a snowy mountain. I told them to hold their hands in front of their eyes and look at the sky. How big was their hand? As big as the sky. Many comparisons, I said, sounded wrong but were actually right in some way. I asked them to compare little things to big things: a mouse is like an elephant; and things in school to things outside school: the blackboard is as green as the sky. I asked them to compare two things that they thought were not alike at all and then see what they felt about it: rain is like a cemetery.

To make things clearer, in the primary, third, and fourth grades I printed LIKE and AS in big letters on the blackboard and told the children to include one in each line. I suggested a repeating form, as I had for the Wish Poem: one comparison in every line.

Some children identified the unusual comparisons I suggested with paradoxes, which in some cases led to extraordinary perceptions: "My skin is as red as a white rose," "The flag is as red, white, and blue as the sun's reflection" (Marion Mackles).

I was pleased but puzzled by Tara Housman's line "A cat is as striped as an airplane takeoff," and I asked her what had made her think of it. "Oh, you know," she told me, "when the plane is on the ground and starts going faster and faster over those white lines on the runway it looks like my cat."

I had the sixth graders write a series of one-line comparisons, which accounts for the presence of their very short works in this section.

Noises

Primary Grade

The Things I Hear in the City

I hear traffic
I hear the Bronx bridge
When I ride on it
I hear cats go mew
I hear yelling.

   Andrea Dockery

I hear at the zoo, like r-r-r-r-r-r-r! And: mo-o-o-o-o!
I hear snakes go ps-s-s-s-s-s-s-s-s

                    Oscar Marcilla

I hear at night somebody snoring
I hear the birds singing in the morning
in the country. A cat goes pr-r-r-r-r.
A sheep goes ba-a-h-a-ha.

Lynne Reiff

I hear birds shripping shrip, shrip.
I hear the traffic honk, honk.
The fire truck goes Ee-e-e-e-e.

Myrna Diaz

Talk talk talk. I
hear people talking.
Toot toot toot toot
the boat goes toot.

Berton Salib

What Do You Hear in the City

I hear my mother cooking beans they go ka-pluk ka-pluk
    ka-pluk

David Jeanpierre

A fire engine goes eeeeeeeeeeee.
A car goes beep, beep.
A cat goes purr, purr.

Melissa Blitz

What I hear on the street
I hear cars that go beep
beep. I hear people that
talk and talk

Alex Morrison

I hear clap when I go to sleep.
I hear a cat going p-p-p
The cats go m-m-m-m.
The bus goes p-p-p-p-p-p
The babies go w-w-w-w-w

Jennie Ortiz

Cracker) Crack, Crack, Crack.
Car) Beep, Beep, Beep.
Cat) Mew, Mew, Mew.
Hands) Cly, Cly, Cly.
Snapping) Snap, Snap, Snap.
Song) Mea- Mea- Mea.
) E-e-e-e-e.

Alicia Lucas

a cat goes mewmew mewmew
a car goes PPPPPPPPPPPPPPP

Valerie Chassé

When I am in bed I hear cars beeb
When I am in school I hear people talking hello goodbye
When I am at home I hear my brother
W-h-h-h-h-h-y
When I am outside I hear the dogs woff-woff

Markus Niebanck

The cat goes prpr prprprp
The dog goes rrrrrr
The pipe goes ssssssss

Leda Mesen

Cars p p. B.r.r.r.r.r.r.r.r. m.m.m.m.
S.s.s.s.s.s. G.r.r.r.r.
at night I hear mouses
H.hh.h.h. m.m.m.m.m.
N.n.n.n.n.n.n.n. O.o.o.o.o.o.o.
B.b.b.b.b.b. prr zzz Eeee
FFFF moooo Boooo

Zaida Rivera

111

I hear a book when it go
plonk. I hear a cat when it go
m-m-m-m-m-m. I hear a dog
When it go g-r-r-r
The car beep beep
A baby go w-w-w-w-w

Author unknown

Booooo in class Spencer
Beep beep beep car
Mea Mea Mea cat
R-r-r-r-r-r-r tiger
CoCoCoCo train.

Author unknown

Monster g-r-r-r-r-r
Booooooo in class.
Screaming E-e-e -e-e-e
Car, P-e-e-e -e-e
Cat, Mew-Mew-Mew-Mew

Carmen Berrios

Fourth Grade

I hear the car go honk-honk.
The dog went to the hog and said you little dog and the hog
    said you are a dog not me.
I hear the people go quark-quark.
I hear the drum go bum-bum.
I hear the piano go be-be.
I hear the mice go squeak-squeak.
The cat sat on the mat and the cat said meor-meor.
I heard a bird go go-go.
The Monkees sound like donkeys.

Ruby Johnson

The Noise I Hear at Night

The beeping cars beeping down the street
The stars go twinkle twinkle in the sky
The dog downstairs going bark bark bark
The cat upstairs going me—row me—row
The bird in my house singing all night.

Lenora Calanni

Sounds

The hot horse went happity-hoppity down the hill
The great, groovy looking girl bought glittering, gleaming go-go boots that made the men go ga-ga
The bright and beaming Betty Barber has a blue pencil that goes bleak-bleak
Mrs. Wendy White did her wash in the wash washy washing machine.

Melanie Popkin

The children sounded like a piano playing.
The rain sounded like a bee coming to play a game. The rain sounded like someone taking a bath.
The street sounded like cars coming from the zoo. The cars sounded like the animals going to a playground.

Maria Teresa Rivera

Owl go like who and who. Who and who and who. And
people go like every time shout out shout out all the
time.

Maria A. Rivera

Noises I Have Heard

The clickey clackey cow went moo-moo when the clickey
clackey train went choo-choo
When the clickey-clackey boat went toot-toot
And all the people said Boo-who.

Mary Minns

I hear the drum go boing-boing-boing, in the bang.
I hear the turkey go grp-grp-grp.
The squeak of the door is like a fast car turning the corner.

Anthony Gomes

Noises I Hear

Clump, clump I won't take out my dump
Boo hoo I won't take out my shoes
Squishy squashy it sounds wishy washy
The busy bees buzzed down Avenue B
The cars clammed like a clown, clowning around
The piano banged like a baby boo hooing
The pages rattled like the guns in a battle
The harp sounded like a dingaling bell
The tapping and the rapping of the ruler tapping
The closing of the notebook sounded like the big bass drum
The sun had the glare of glass in it
The red glare was like the red in the flag.

Annie Clayton

The big bad baby bus came busy bussing down Avenue B. The big round clock went thump dump. The big cookaraca cook down Cooky Street. The big bad pants lay faded on the chair. The two class clashing hands clashing against the clashing wall. The rock and roll. Roll rock came ricking and rocking to rock.

Eduardo Diaz

Sleepness

The bigness of my brother goes flought
And he slips on some water kaslashel
He falls down the stairs fink fankel fump
Fump
But when he's asleep hok ssssss hok sssssss

He experiments with powder ka-pla ka-pla
And he works at Con Ed cack cack cack cack
He goes to the bathroom gra gra gra gra
But that terrible noise hok ssss hok sssss

Charles Conroy

I was looking out the window and I heard ding dong coming
     from the church
And the cars went zoom as they passed by
I smelled something so I sniffed it it was nothing but cookies
I live near the ocean so I heard the waves swishing
Ring went the bikes on the street
Crack went the hammer against the wall
Tick tock went the grandfather in the hall
The fly buzzed by me near the window
I heard the train going too-too when it stopped by the station
At night I heard the wind howling at the window
         dong dong
       dong dong dong
       dong dong dong
       dong dong dong
       time to go to bed

Marion Mackles

Fifth Grade

I wore a bathing suit that clashed and then I dashed and
     splashed in the water.
The girl started to swing on the swing, and started to sing.
When the rock'n'roll group began to sing, the children began
     to swing.

Debbie Novitsky

Sounds

The birds chirp when the chip-off-the-old-block fox comes
    along.
The mooey chooey cow ate the mooey chooey grass.
The honky bonky horns of cars honk away.
The swishy swashy splashy water goes splashy swishy swashy.

Ana Gomes

Sounds I Heard

I heard whistles whistling with a policeman policeing the beep-
    ing horns
I heard a flute fluting a race with a low tuba
I heard an elephant jumping up and down that sounded like
    thumping drum
I heard a lion lioning the other lions
I heard a radio radioing its brains out.

Gloria Peters

Click, Click, Click I clicked out the cracked clashy lights
Swish Swish I clean my shelf while drinking Welch's grapejuice
Pit Pit Pit the wit was a hit like a dit
Dit dot dit the telegraph goes dit dot
Spursh, spursh, goes the water hose.

Amy Levy

The eraser scratched the back of the pad.
The crunched paper sounded like a crunch of a bunch of
    lunch.
The flute sounded high as the cry of a whistle.
The bell sounded well when I fell in a cell.
A clink sounds like a drink of pink water.

Alan Constant

I smashed into the splashy waves.
The glass smashed cracked on the floor.
I slide down the slide.
The flute fluted like a bird.
The clarinet cluttered at me.

Natalie De Stefano

My crazy cousin drove the clickity clankity car down the street.
I shot my short shirt out the window of a shooting star.
Chimmey Chummy chirped like the camp of a chippy chappy
    championship.
Arley's airplane is apt to abbreviate your apple.
The pink petunias turned purple from pumping pipes.

Ruben Marcilla

Sixth Grade

The City

The fire engine's bell goes ting-a-ling, ling
A man shutting his car door goes whack
A little kid crying mama!
The garbagemen collecting the day's trash is bang bang
Men and women slushing slushing in the gutter water
The window washer and his brush go swish swish
And the milkman's gay friendly whistle

Emilia Scifo

I hear the Superball
That's bouncing and bouncing
"Boing," "boing," it went into the street
"Zoom," "put," "put," a taxi knocked it down the block

I chased after it and "slush"
I fell into a puddle
Down the sewer it went
With a "splash" and then it boinged up again

Down the block I ran
With a "clash," "clash," "clash"
In that puddle again
I fell down with a "swap"

I finally got tired and stopped
And sat on the bench
Then I heard a little "boing" "boing" from far off
And before I knew it, it fell in front of my feet
With a "swoosh" plus a little "boing."

Eric Sebbane

Form a circle with your mouth
Blow out air
And there you create the sound of a lonely wind on the
    English moors

Bang a ruler on a chair
And there you create
The clattering of the hip boots of the Nazi S.S.

If you clap your hands
Flesh meeting flesh
You create the sound of a slap

A baby's cry
Will warn of disaster
It sounds like an air raid
So you better beware!

Close a window
And you will hear a file cabinet closing

Chalk on a blackboard
And you will create the squeaking of brakes.

Author unknown

When I'm in the street I hear a car's horn being blown the sound sunds like a kong or pa-pa and when I'm in bed I hear kind of a high pitch it sounds like eeeeeeee. When my friend yells it sounds like a person falling off a cliff or something going to fall on them it sounds like Ahhhhhhhh. Sometimes when I'm in bed it sounds like a million bats and I could hear them screech.

Ramon Rivera

The wind coming out of your mouth
Is like the wind in a dark alley
When you hear older people talking
You hear groaning
Hitting a chair with a ruler
Is like hearing a machine gun fire
Hearing a dog whine
Is like a fire truck's siren
Seeing two boxers connect with a punch
Is like a bullet hitting a tin can

Evan Steinberg

Traffic

The sound of horns sounds like the striking of a xylophone
The noises of brakes sound like the screeching of a rooster
The sound of the motors makes me think of a ferocious lion
The sound of fast-moving cars sounds like the rushing water
    hitting the land

Author unknown

A yoyo sounds like a bearing rubbing in a machine,
A bicycle sounds like a small suction cup coming off the wall,
And a roller skate sounds like a light sledge hammer hitting
    a concrete wall.
A toy gun sounds like a caveman pounding a flint.

Roberto Marcilla

Noises

Sound is an important part of poetry, and the Noise Poems I gave my students seemed a good, simple way to start them thinking about it. I asked them to do two things: make sound comparisons (say what sounds like what), and write whole lines that imitated a particular sound ("The clink was like a drink of pink water").

I did what I could in class to help them associate sounds freely with other things and find enjoyable sound comparisons. I crumpled up a piece of paper, dropped a bunch of keys on the floor, and asked them what those things sounded like. (Somebody typing. Bells ringing.) To help them associate words with sounds I did two things: I began with an onomatopoetic word and asked for other words that sounded like it; and I made a noise (I hit a chair back with a ruler) and asked them what *words* that sounded like. For the first I used the sound a bee makes: buzz. I asked for other words that sounded like a bee but whose meaning didn't have anything to do with buzz. The children found some quickly: fuzz, does, was, cousin, muzzle. When I hit the chair, the children said the word it sounded like was *hit*. I asked for another word for *hit*, and they said *tap*. I asked them to close their eyes and tell me which of those two words the noise was most like, then I hit the chair again. Most agreed it sounded more like *tap*. I asked them to close their eyes again and try to hear a word in the noise which didn't have anything to do with the meaning of *tap*. They heard *hat*, *snap*, *back*, *cat*. Once they were thinking in this way about sounds I had them write the poems.

I gave the Noise Poem to the sixth graders first and I hadn't yet thought of the entire-line sound imitation, so I just asked them to do sound comparisons. I asked the primary graders for sound comparisons and for how things "went" (the cow goes maaaaa). I asked fourth and fifth graders to do both sound comparisons and entire lines that imitated a sound. In giving the poem to the fourth graders I read some poems by Wallace Stevens.

The children enjoyed writing about sounds, and sounds frequently came into the poems they wrote afterwards. Writing Noise Poems puts a certain zip into children's work and might be a good thing to have them do once every term.

Dreams

Fourth Grade

Dream

I dream of many colors making a pattern.
I clutter my mind with arithmetic examples.
I try to play piano in my sleep.
I dream that every day is October ninth.
I dream that I have a golden throne.
I dream I have all the clothes I want.
I dream that there won't be any school tomorrow.
I dream I'm in the movies.
I dream I'm standing on the floor and diamonds snow on me.
I dream I know all the Bob Dylan songs my brother knows.
I dream all my boyfriends date me and not my friends.
I dream that every year I have my weight in gold.

Annie Clayton

My Conversation With the Sky

Once I walked up to the Sky and said, "Hi, Sky. What are
   you doing?"
"Oh, just hanging around. It is rather boring," said the Sky.
"One thing, Sky. I thought you couldn't fly. Is it still true?"
"Definitely. Why do you ask such stupid questions?"
"Well, I hate to ask this next question, but if that is true,
   how do you stay up there?"
The Sky didn't answer, because he was falling down to earth!

Lisa Jill Braun

My Dream

I had a dream that I was in a forest
The trees grabbed me and tried to eat me
I kicked them all and ran away
Then I fell in a flower garden
I fell in a flower the flower closed
I was trying to get out of the flower
Then I woke up and found myself in bed instead of a flower

Lenora Calanni

A Dream

I went down a winding staircase
And saw people who all were stars.
The staircase didn't go all the way down
So I had to jump a little of the way.

Then all the people looked like fish
With small tails and smaller bodies
And one led me up a different staircase
That also had steps that went around.

He led me to a door and told me to go in
And said it was a house with a lot of rooms
And also not to go into the kitchen,
And left me there.

I went into the house and found the kitchen
And went in and saw a big, big cat.
And on the wall were big chunks of raw meat
About two feet long.

The cat was very thin and hungry
And was bleeding on its back
I fed it a big chunk of meat but—
It wanted more.

I gave it more and more and more
And finally it wasn't hungry.
I let it loose from the chain it was tied up on
And it started to purr.

It rubbed against me so hard
That it knocked me down
It started to eat me but I woke up
With my cat on me going to sleep.

Erin Harold

Dreams

I dreamed I had a dog.
I dreamed it was the nicest and prettiest dog on earth.
The dog had a lot of hair. The hair was very baggy.
I dreamed I loved him and I would all my life.
I dreamed he died and I was very, very sad.
I dreamed in the dream that I woke up.
I dreamed that it was all a dream.
I dreamed I had a cat but I didn't want to
Dream any more if the dream was like the other one.

Marion Mackles

A Dream

I had a dream of a speeding car going beep-beep while a train
    goes choo-choo,
A noisy owl goes woo-woo with its small hair tail on its head,
Also Hey! diddle-diddle with the cat in his fiddle
The bells of a fire engine go wee-wee while the cannons go
    Boom.

Ruben Luyando

Dreams

One day I dreamed that a ghost was going to take me.
And one day I dreamed that an elephant was going to eat me.
One day I dreamed that my mother was going to buy me a
    cast in pine.
And one day I dreamed that I was in a cave with a lion.

Elizabeth Cabán

The Mind

The killer is on the loose and he's tired
The killer jumps off the cliff and lands on a mind
He says stomp stomp with his feet
To try to mush this mind
He goes kasedel and lands on the top of a mountain
He thinks with his foot about this mush
He jumps off the mountain and kisses it.

Charles Conroy

Dreams

I love to dream about cows that go moo.
I love to dream about horses that go raaaaa.
I love to dream about sheep that go baa.
I love to dream about fish that go burp.
I love to dream about cars that go honk.
I love to dream about trucks that go beep.

Theamando Zaharias

Beauty of the Forest

I was in the most beautiful place in the world. It was called the place of beauty hillside. I went walking through the sunny hillside and then I came to a hill that was all frosty white and there was a beautiful castle made of green and yellow stones and a white diamond on the top of the castle. And in the background there was the most beautiful rainbow of the color of pink, white, red, blue and green. And when I woke up I was so gay. But I will never forget that beautiful sight.

Vivien Tuft

Dream Poem

Once I had a dream that my friend was a carrot and I was a
    cucumber.
I was never eaten neither was my friend.
We sat in a store ready to be bought.
So one day I ran and ran until I got out of the store. But I
    forgot about my friend.
So I ran back and tried to call my friend
And tell her to come but she couldn't hear me
So I ran back in the store and I almost got stepped on but
    the lady with her shoe kicked me. I fell right back in the
    carrot pile and I learned if you're a fruit don't run away
    or you'll get eaten anyway.

Ilona Baburka

I Really Dreamed

We went to Kentucky in the winter. I went down to Rex's to get my pony Cricket. Then I attached her to a sled and I drove her to New York. Then in my dream I woke up and found it was all a dream but then I saw Cricket nuzzling me. The President put a grass field in our backyard. I entered Cricket in a trick show and she won first prize for walking upstairs on her hind legs.

Eliza Bailey

Fifth Grade

A Dream

I once dreamed
That I lived on
A planet full of peace
One dare not say
A word about
The violence there had been
The flowers bloomed
Yet never wilted
The people they were gay
But that was a dream
No wars or meanness,
But that was a dream.

Amy Levy

Sleepy Dream

I dreamt I went to school in my blue and white pajamas.
I took three pink pillows and fell asleep during a social stud-
     ies lesson.
My friends slept with me. Two to each pink pillow.
No more pink pillows so poor Mrs. Weick must sleep on that
     horrible social studies book.
We dreamt we went to school in our blue and white, orange
     and yellow, and psychedelic pajamas.

Robin Harold

Expo 67

I had a dream that school was over
I was at Expo 67
I was on a bright blue train
Sitting next to a fake Mickey Mouse
I went through different pavilions of thoughts
I went through mushroom clouds of an atomic bomb, a paper
     submarine half-filled with water
I saw a clock whose minute hand told the hour and an hour
     hand that told the minute. Everyone was changing his
     watch.
I looked down and saw a waterfall with diamond fish floating
     downstream
Then I saw a friend and that is all I remember

Joel London

Dreams

Dreams, like wishes, are a frequent source of poetic inspiration. Having children write about them is an easy way to make them aware of their unconscious experience and to encourage them to bring it into their poems. Children can write about dreams directly, as if they really happened, and they enjoy doing it—even the scary parts.

The poem can be assigned in different ways. One can ask the children to write about a dream they remember, or one can ask them to go home and dream and be ready to write about it the next day. If children didn't remember their dreams of the night before, I told them to write about their favorite dream or dreams, or the dream they thought about most.

I would suggest doing the Dream Poem after the children have written poems using wishes, comparisons, sounds, and maybe even lies and colors. The more thematic and sensuous material they have experience in using, the more they will be able to put into the description of their dreams. I had the sixth graders write Dream Poems before they had done any of these others, and the poems turned out a little flat and empty.

I didn't suggest any form for this poem, but many used versions of the repeating form of previous poems. A form could be suggested, such as starting every line with "I dreamed," or putting the word "dream" in every line, but if the poem were a narration such repetition might interrupt it too much.

Wishes, Noises, Dreams and Comparisons Together

Fourth Grade

My Dream

I had a dream with everything brown.
The trees were brown as dark as brown.
I heard a sound going moo, moo, boo, boo.
It was a cow who wanted a wife.
The cow was dark brown as a crayon brown.
I went to the barn I saw him booing (and mooing)
I looked up in the sky and saw something.
I saw the moon it was brown too.
My mother came down she was brown too.
When my father came he was brown too.
It was a brown day.
Everyone was singing brown, brown, and brown.
And the cow mooing and mooing again.

Tomas Torres

The Noise of the Breeze

The noise of the breeze goes click click.
The breeze floats through the gleaming sky.
The birds fly by the fields and farms.
The squirrel runs under a bright red apple tree.
Then I fall asleep and dream that I was a king.
I was dreaming that I was a king on a throne.
The throne was made of pure gold and silver.
Then I woke up and in a little while
I wish that I were the strongest boy.
I wish that I were rich with gold and money.
I wish that I have a good long life.

Luis Scifo

Wishes and Dreams

I wish planes had motors that went rum bang zingo and would
be streaming green as the sea.
I wish the moon would crash down on the sun and would
blow up like caps in a cap bomb shell.
I had a dream that the world would freeze to an ice cube and
when the sun came close would melt to water, and would
drip down through the universe.
I dreamed of having a space ship and would zoom through
the galaxy at the speed of sound and it would go bang
squeak and scratch.

Argentina Wilkinson

My Sounding Dream

I had a clinging dream about a clanging car
The clanging car was the Mach Five
While I was going down the road I wished it wouldn't go
    cling clang
The next day I found the reason that troubled me
Soon it got so loud it sounded like an angry lion
After a day or two I fixed it
The next day it sounded like a crying baby
But that I like so I left it like that

Martin Freihofer

The Contrary Women

Once there was a lady who made trouble everywhere
And had trouble setting her very witchy hair
She took off her nose that was made of skaslup putty
I wish that contrary women never existed
I dream about these women
But there is no doubt
That dream would scare you
    Into a million parts.

Charles Conroy

Wish Sound Comparison Poem

I wish I had a piano that goes ting ting
I wish I had a dog that goes wolf wolf
As red as an apple on an apple tree
As hot as hot sauce in your mouth
Choo choo beep beep Zoommmm planes trains trucks

Iris Torres

Country Screams

Sometimes I wish I'd have good dreams
And all of them would come true
We'd have a car that would go beep beep,
And move into the country

And the buzzing of bees would mean a jump
Under a bed so gracelessly
And this act would be performed
By my big sister, "eekingly"

And a wasp is a very loud scream
To be heard for miles around
And the tiniest ant would make a scream
By my sister, what an ear-piercing sound.

"And these big bad buzzing bees came,
So I jumped underneath a bed.
And it was such a ferocious swarm," says sister
But of course it was only one.

Erin Harold

Wishes, Noises, Dreams and Comparisons Together

This poem combined the themes of the last four poems the children had written. It seemed a good way to encourage them to use together the different things they were trying out and learning. To get them in the mood for writing it, I read aloud some of their Dream Poems which contained wishes, noises, and comparisons.

Any number of combination poems might work well: for example, Colors and Lies; Colors and Lies and Noises; an I Used To/But Now Poem written while listening to music.

Metaphors

Fourth Grade

The pretzel is a Mrs. Wiener.
The rose is a ripe cherry.
The wasp is a scream from my big sister.
A bee is a jump underneath the bed by my sister.
A cloud is a kitten playing with a breeze.
A breeze is a string for a cloud to play with.
Is the sun a ball of string which the breeze was cut from?
Maybe, but the breeze is blue and the sun is orange.
Do the cloud cats drink the rain?
Maybe, but do they like it?
No, because it isn't milk.

Erin Harold

The rain falling from the sky is tears from a little girl's eyes.
Salt falling to the food is snow falling to the ground.

Melanie Popkin

Run Appalosa Run!

The plants are the shadow of the Jolly Green Giant
Mr. Koch is a very well-dressed poetry book walking around in
    shining shoes.

Tara Housman

The light is a seagull
Mrs. Wiener is a pretzel she is worth two cents
The dog is a door opening and closing
The book is a written reindeer
The yellow letter is a moon.

Anthony Gomes

The Sick Flag

The blue in the flag is a boy with chickenpox
The red and white on a flag is a cut with blood rolling out
The stick holding up the flag is the spear that made the cut
And altogether the flag is certainly a sick one.

Martin Freihofer

Blank is a Blank

The snow is a snowflake.
The blue sky is an ocean.
The blackboard is a black notebook.
An apple is a red rose.
A bat is a big fat stick.
Mrs. Wiener is a lovely flower which shouts.

Tomas Torres

The Fruit Bowl

A nose is a banana except it is
                    Yellow
A head is a pumpkin except it is
                    Orange
A cheek is an apple except it has a
                    Stem
A body is a fruit bowl because it has
                    Everything

Charles Conroy

Metaphors

I told the children to think about a thing being like something else (the cloud is like a pillow) and to pretend that it really was the other thing; thus, to say IS instead of IS LIKE (the cloud is a pillow). Then, if they liked, they could elaborate on this one metaphor (I rest my head on the cloud) for the entire poem (as Martin Freihofer does in "The Sick Flag"), or start a new metaphor in every line. Metaphors are a good, enjoyable experience for children, though they are a little difficult. They are harder than comparisons, and I'd suggest giving them after rather than before the Comparison Poem. It was just an accident that I gave this poem only to the fourth grade class. I'd like to try it with others.

The Mrs. Wiener/pretzel metaphors are due to the fact that Mrs. Wiener, the fourth-grade teacher, was fond of pretzels; the children, having seen her eating them, took this occasion to tease her by identifying her with them.

A Swan of Bees

Third Grade

I Would Like To Have

I would like to have a door of hearts
I would like to have a room of roses
I would like to have a window of flowers
I would like to have a book of stripes
I would like to have a desk of red strawberries
I would like to have a boat of kittens
I would like to have a surfboard of daisies
I would like to have a pocketful of bows
I would like to have a pillow full of air
I would like to have a brush full of spots
I would like to have a name full of designs
I would like to have a tree full of money.

Ilona Baburka

Someday I Hope to See

Someday I hope to see a face with roses
A hat of kisses
A stripe of hair
A kiss of babies
An eraser of kittens
A baby of mittens
A lady of decks
A helper of scientists
A post office of babies
A skeleton of discoveries
A carton of stages
A map of pictures
A library of stripes
A person of books
A name of brushes

Mayra Morales

I have a light made out of grapefruit
I'll give you a head of peaches
I have a hat made of bugs
An airplane made of bananas
An innard made out of roses
A man made of shoes
A head made of bicycles
A bay made of money
A house made of candy

Stephen Sebbane

149

Strange Things

A window of roses is like the 50 stars in the United States flag
A house of flags from all the flags all over the world
My head is as big as the world
A river of the color red and real shiny

Arnaldo Gomez

Strange Things

A blackboard of moons
A window of kisses
A flag of boxes
A swimming pool of doorknobs
A shirt made of tulips
A heart of squares
A teacher made out of hearts
A man made out of balloons
A girl made out of popcorn
A boat made out of clocks
A girl made out of kittens.

Jeannie Turner

Odd Things

A shirt of beads
A flag of water
A door of windows
A person made of toys
A flower made of a person
A bed made of light
A skeleton of coat hangers
A paper made of wood
A building made of plastic
A ball made of cement
A letter made of words.

Billy Battina

I Had a

I had a dream of my banana pillow
and of my pyjamas of oranges.
I had another dream of my
breakfast of giraffes and my
dinner of skeletons.
I have a blackboard of hair
and my T.V. of dresses.

Madelyn Mattei

Somebody Gave Me

Somebody gave me a paper of dresses
Somebody gave me a hair of colors
Somebody gave me a rose of roses
My mother gave me a skeleton of skin
Somebody gave to me a shirt of stories
Somebody gave to me the sky made of sugar
My sister gave to me the lights of hearts
I got the chair of red
Somebody gave to me a sock of chocolate

Mercedes Mesen

I have a pocket full of laughs,
I have a dog of dreams,
I have a hat made of checkers,
I have a school bag made of crayons,
I was given a dress of shoes,
I have a sailboat of sinking water.
I have a house of candy,
I was given a piece of paper made of roses,
I have a red blue and white striped rose.

Eliza Bailey

A Hat of Laughs

I have a hat
Full of laughs
A book of kisses
A coke came out
Like Mr. Coke
A monkey jumped out
As a hat full of money came out
Somebody gave me a red
White and blue flag
As it hit the tank
A pig jumped out
A camel jumped out
As he was a scout
A horse jumped out
A cat jumped out
An old lady jumped out
With a seesaw hat
Out comes a rat
Out comes a sack
Out comes me
Out comes you

Fontessa Moore

I saw a fancy dancy dress
hanging on a fancy dancy window
of red roses you could call it a red
rose window I put it on and I
danced to a swan of bees I put
it on a chair of rock and I looked
at the sky of hand I put on
my fancy dancy dress I fell
asleep and I had a dream
of a blue sky of roses and a
house of daisies

and I awoke and it was true
I saw everything I saw
sky of roses house of daisies a tree
of orange a book of apple and
I loved it all and I lived with it for
the rest of my life

Marion Mackles

A Swan of Bees

This idea came from a third-grade Comparison Poem in which *swarm* was misspelled *swan*. The accidental compound, "swan of bees," seemed to me interesting and even exciting, and I thought that if it appealed to the third graders also I would have them write a poem with a lot of such objects in it. They liked the "swan of bees," so I gave them a few more examples of the phenomenon—a window of kisses, a blackboard of dreams—and asked them for some. When everyone had caught on, I asked for a poem in which there was a swan-of-bees-type object in every line. To help them with form I said they could if they liked start every line with a phrase such as "I wish I had" or "I once saw." Their teacher, Mrs. Schapiro, printed a big OF on the blackboard to help them remember what they were supposed to do. The idea was a success, and interesting swan-of-bees phenomena also turned up in the Used To/But Now poems, which were the next ones they wrote.

There are other ways to present this idea; it is really the elementary idea of form and content: a poem of words, a table of wood. The swan of bees had a certain advantage in being fantastic: it made the children think of strange and wonderful combinations. One could begin by giving some examples with objects in the room. By picking up a world globe, for instance, and asking the children what strange substance it might be made of. Or the children can be told they own a magical factory where anything can be manufactured out of anything else: they can make a hat of dreams, an automobile of words, a boat of chalk.

I Used To / But Now

Primary Grade

I used to be a fish
But now I am a nurse
I used to read *My City*
But now I am up to *Round The Corner*
I used to be as silly as David
But now I am sillier than David

Andrea Dockery

I used to write sloppy but now I write better.
I used to be in fourth grade now I am in sixth grade.
I used to be in high school
But now I have a good education.

Jennie Ortiz

I used to live in New Jersey
But now I live in New York.
I didn't have a little brother before
But now I do!
I used to dream of racing cars
But now I dream of super heroes.
I used to have a funny book
But now I don't have it.
I used to eat grass, but now I eat flowers because they are
     sweet.
I used to drive trucks, but now I drive racing cars.
I used to be in first grade
But now I'm in second grade.

Oscar Marcilla

I used to be a baby
But now I am a big girl
I used to be a pest
But now I am nice
I used to be a bad little girl
But now I'm a good girl
I used to have black shoes
But now they don't fit me
I used to play
But now I don't play
I used to fight
But now I don't.

Valerie Chassé

I used to dream of being a fireman.
But now I dream of being a racer.
I used to be littler than a sugar bag.
But now I'm bigger.
I used to read *My City*.
But now I read *Round the Corner*.

Berton Salib

I look like a monkey in a tree
I used to be stupid last year
But now I am smart
I look like a black cow
I used to be in second grade
But now I am in third grade
But now I am little then I am big
I was bad but now I'm good

Zaida Rivera

I used to play bowling but now I play baseball.
Before I didn't know what two plus two was but now I do.
Before I didn't go to school.
But before I didn't know Steven.

Robert Mattei

I used to have an apple dress,
But now it doesn't fit me.
I used to have black sneakers,
But now they don't fit me.
I used to have a blue coat,
But now it doesn't fit me.

Myrna Diaz

I used to be smart
But now I'm smarter
I used to be pretty
But now I'm prettier
I used to be little
But now I'm bigger

Agnes Minns

Third Grade

I Used To Be

I used to be a desk but now I'm a pencil
I used to be hair but now I'm a head
I used to be a fish but now I'm a girl
I used to be a person but now I'm a dope
I used to be the sky but now I'm the ground
I used to dance but now I'm a statue
I was a square but now I'm a circle
I used to be a rose but now I'm a leaf
I used to be a boy and now I'm a woman
I used to have a baby but now he's a dog
I used to be a rope but now I jump
Yesterday Mr. Koch was a man and today he's a boy
I used to be a cow but now I'm a horse
I used to be a paper but today I'm made of wood
I used to be big but now I'm large

Mercedes Mesen

When I lived in Texas I wanted to be big now I live in New
    York I want to be a baby.
When I was in second grade I used to think school was fun
    but now I am in third grade I think school is a bore.
I used to be a pig but now I am a hog.
Yesterday I was looking for my banana coat now I am looking
    for my dress of apples.

Eliza Bailey

I Used To But Now ✓

I used to want to be a baseball player with my brother
But now I want to be a dancer
I used to want to be a singer
But now I want to be a dancer
I used to want to be a model
But now I want to be a dancer
I used to want to be a queen
But now I want to be a dancer
I used to want to be a dressmaker
But now I want to be a dancer
I used to want to be a boy
But now I want to be a dancer
I used to want to be a pen
But now I want to be a dancer
I used to want to be a king
But now I want to be a dancer

Marion Mackles

Last year I was for baseball now I go for football
I used to say bow
But now I say wow
I used to be brown
But since I saw a house I turned white
I saw a red doll and feel I am red
But that was a dream
I dropped my pencil last year
But this year I pick it up
I am blue this year
But this year I am black.

Thomas Kennedy

I used to be a baseball player with a purple ball
But now I go skating with a red and white giraffe
I used to dream of nice devils
But now I dream of evil angels
I used to see a bow tie with white and red cigars
But now I see a noisy little cigar
I used to be a giraffe
But now I'm a baby giraffe
I used to be Mr. Pepsi
But now I'm Mr. Gingerale
I used to be a mailman with a happy little letter
But now I am a policeman with red and white shoes

Michael Freihofer

Dopey Things

I used to be eight years old
But now I am nine
I used to have diapers
But now I have underwear
I used to have a blue dress
But now I have a pink dress
I used to be a man
But now I am a woman
I used to be a baby saying Coo Coo
But now I say "Hello"
I used to be a goldfish
But now I am a girl.

> *Lisa Smalley*

I Used to But Now

I used to like the Beatles
But now I like the Monkees
I used to have a white eraser
But now I have a black eraser
I used to have a dress of roses
But now I have a dress of apples
I used to have a teacher of meanness
But now I have a teacher of roses

> *Maria Ippolito*

Wishes

I used to be a green frog
But now I am a black fish
I used to be a white shoe
But now I am a black sock
I used to be a red, white and blue flag
But now I am a yellow dress
I used to be a pair of sunglasses
But now I am a pair of bland glasses
I used to be a drawing paper
But now I am a loose leaf paper
I used to be a book
But now I am a newspaper
I used to be a desk
But now I am a chair
I used to be the world
But now I am the globe

Esther Garcia

I Used To Be

Three years ago I used to be six years old
But now I am eight years old
Four years later I used to be so cute then I got so ugly
I used to be small
But now I'm tall
And that is all
I used to be strong
But now I am so lazy
I used to be a baby
But now I'm not
I'm a tall person
Like an ordinary one
I don't doubt on it
But now I'm in the third grade
I used to be a pig
But now I'm Fontessa

Fontessa Moore

I Used To But Now

I used to be a flower but now I'm a color
I used to be a brush but now I'm a strawberry
I used to be a person but now I'm a pocket
I used to be a book but now I'm a ladybug
I used to be a design but now I'm a tree
I used to be an eraser but now I'm a pencil
I used to be a clown but now I'm a chimney
I used to be a bow but now I'm a dot
I used to have a hat of hearts but now I have a hat of tears
I used to have a dress of buttons but now I have a name of
    bees
I used to have a dot but now I have a rose of measles
I used to have a picture but now I have a strip
I used to have a book of dreams but now I have a name of
    eyes
I used to have teeth of black but now I have teeth of yellow
I used to have a ladybug but now I have a picture of people.

Ilona Baburka

A Colorful Dream

I used to be a nurse
But now I am a dead person
I always was Mr. Coke
But now I am Mrs. Seven Up

I wish I had a peanut
But now I wish I had a doll
I wish I were in first grade
But now I am in nursery school

I am a pink
But now I am a yellow, pink
I used to be a glass
But now I am a cup

I wish I were a king
But I am a rock
I used to make cakes to eat
But now I make mudpies to eat.

Thomas Rogaski

I used to be a baby
But now I am a grown-up
I used to be a fish
But now I am big
I used to be a funny baby
But now I am a sad grown-up
I used to have little dresses
But now I have big ones
I used to drink in a bottle
But now I drink in a glass
I used to be in a carriage
But now I am in a car
I used to walk slow
But now I walk fast.

Ileana Mesen

Fourth Grade

Long Ago

Once I had a lot of nice friends but now I have only six—
   three girls and three boys.
I used to have a lot of guns but now only six ones.
I used to like to play with girls but now I play with the boys
   in the country.
I used to speak a lot of German but now I speak only half of
   what I used to.
I used to like a boy but now he's moved away to Germany, he
   still writes to me and I write to him but I never see him.

Argentina Wilkinson

Last Time and This Time

When I was a baby I had no pets.
Now I have three pets.
When I was a baby I couldn't swim, I couldn't even play.
When I was a baby I wore baby clothes but little clothes.
And now I wear big clothes like size 12½.
When I was a baby I went to bed early.
And now I go to bed at 10:00 in the night.
When I was a baby my mother and father loved me,
But now love and hate me sometimes.
I just like both. Do you? I just like both.
When I was a baby I looked so pretty,
But now just forget me.
When I was a baby I couldn't play,
I couldn't play because somebody might get hurt and you
        know who.
But now I am strong, and I am glad I am me. Are you? I'm
        just glad.

Tomas Torres

Now and Then

I used to have blonde curly hair
Now I have brown straight hair.

Things used to be terrible with teachers
Now they are made great with Mrs. Wiener.

I used to have a canary
Now I have a goldfish.

I used to have a goldfish
Now I have none.

I used to have a nice brother
Now he punches me in the shoulder.

I used to have a red velvet dress
Now I have a pink dress with a flowered bottom.

I used to have friends with common names
Now they are a new kind of names.

Annie Clayton

Fifth Grade

I Was, But Now

I used to be a baby who was one, two, three, etc.
But now I am a lady
I used to wear diapers
But now I wear everything—including diamonds, fur coats,
    and those rich stuff
I used to be ugly
But now I'm sexy
I used to wish I was a boy
But now I don't because I found out what boys go through
I used to like eggs
But now the color of the yolk makes me sick
I used to like plaid
But now I like checkers
I used to be young
But now I still am
I Am What I Am

Gloria Peters

That's Odd

I am very unusual. People called me odd and this is why
I used to cry when everyone else laughed
But now I laugh when everyone else cries
I used to be born in 1957
But now I'm born in 1857 because my birth certificate was
    written wrong
I used to be married
But now I'm divorced
Yet today is my sixth birthday
I used to hate a person whose name I don't want to mention
But now I still hate her
I used to throw water balloons
But now I don't because one landed in a place I don't want
    to mention
I used to be able only to scream
But now all I can do is whisper because of a voice defect.

Joel London

I Used To / But Now

This theme is one children love to write about: the difference between the way they are now and the way they used to be. The changes in their lives are big and dramatic and have happened fast. They are bigger every year, they're in a different grade, they have different clothes and new interests, and so on. Adult poems on this theme are usually sad and concerned with loss of love, beauty, and youth; children's poems about the past are sometimes sad too, but more often they have a triumphant note—"I used to be littler than a sugar bag/But now I'm bigger." Younger children often write about radical physical transformations—"I used to be a boy/But now I am a girl."

The suggestion to begin every odd line with "I used to" and every even line with "But now" seemed to help everybody think about past and present in a free and easy way.

If I Were the Snow, and Spring

Fifth and Sixth Grades

Jingle, jingle, jingle
The wind is blowing
The snow is falling
And jingle bells are ringing.
How gay it is, a winter scene on Christmas eve.
Oh, hi, I'm the snow.
I can travel for miles
Around and no one can ever
Hear me. A shining green sleigh
Is clopping up the lane.
I love to fall on it and
On the backs of the horses pulling it.
Everything is getting white.
The horses whinny and neigh
Everything is getting bright
And on the ground I lie.

Natalie De Stefano

If I Were the Snow

If I were the snow
I would snow every
single Christmas.
I would snow on my
brother and make his
toes so red he
would hit me.
I would snow all over the
universe on Mars,
the earth. I would
snow so hard on
the moon, I
would show the man
on there who's boss.
I would not be just white
I'd be red, blue, and
green. I'd be yellow
dots, orange dots
black ones too.

Kathy Kennedy

Berum, Berum, it's cold up here.
What's this? I'm turning to ice.
I'm as hard as a rock.
How uncomfortable I am.
Omygosh I'm falling way down
To the earth, to the ground.
My unlucky friend Sam
Has fallen in the city
I hate it there, so noisy, so dirty
I'm so light, dancing in the air
I'll land in the country
On the nose of a horse
And he'll say, "You mischievous rascal,
But you are some one to talk to"
And now the good horse gives me plenty of rides
Over the hills and through pastures
The horse fell down
Because of the sly fox
And jumped down on the critter
And froze him to death.
And then I melted away.

Jeff Morley

Snow, Snow

Snow, snow, I'm the snow
Drift, drift, far I drift
Friends, friends, with my friends
Deep, deep, deep I drift
In and out, out of windows
Into Paris, out of London
        But!!
Melt, melt, soon I'll melt.
But while I can, can, can
Drift, drift, I will drift
Snow, snow, I'm the snow
Drift, drift, far I drift.
Friends, friends, with my friends
Deep, deep, deep I drift
But now I must MELT!

Amy Levy

What I Would Do If I Was Snow

If I were snow I would fill up the streets
If I were snow I would also freeze my brother
If I were snow I would be mean and nice.
If I were snow and I saw somebody eating
Something very hot I would cool it for him.
But if he was somebody I hate
I would call my friend the wind and tell him
"Wind would you like to do me a favor"
And he would say "Yes, what is it" and I would answer
"Please blow that man down."
My friend the wind is also nice and mean.
If I were snow I would fill up the roofs
And make them look nice and beautiful.
If I were snow I would do more good deeds
        Than bad ones.

Miquel Lopez

I am a snow flake. I always wear white clothes. I am traveling
all over the world. I see things nobody has ever seen. I
could go into people's houses. And then I would just move
on and on and on.

If I were the snow, I would call all of my friends to come to earth
and we would pile up on each other. We would make us
ten inches high and spread all over the world. And we
would cover the sun with clouds so it could not melt us.

Carmine Vinciforo

If I were the snow I would fall on the window ledges so I could
make the buildings look decorated.
If I were the snow I would fall on the ground so the children
could pick me up and throw me into the air.
If I were the snow I would cover all windows so people could
not see what is going on outside.
If they tried to brush me away I would freeze them as fast as I
could.

Ana Gomes

If I Were the Snow

I'd fall on the houses
            the street
            the cars
I'd fall on my friends
            bad people
            the doctor
            the police
            the teachers.
If I was the snow I'd help the children, the safeties.
If I was the snow I'd break a window and go in.
If I was the snow I'd blow the people to their offices.
And blow them through the window.
If I was the snow I'd blow the coats off.
If I was the snow I would blow the houses down.
If I was the snow I'd be bad and sometimes good. I'd blow
      their books to school.
If I was the snow I'd blow them to the park.

                                        Gloria Peters

Fourth Grade

Spring is like a ladybug climbing a flower.
Spring is flowers growing in the garden.
Spring is the sun, sky and grass.
Spring is going to the swimming pool.
Spring is going to the beach and tasting the salt water.
Spring is wearing your new summer play suit.
Spring is planting new flowers in your garden.
Spring is getting a new pair of sandals.

But best of all spring is part of nature, like the baby next door
She's grown so big.

Vivien Tuft

The spring is like polluted air.
When spring comes the flowers die.
Spring is the ugliest season there is.
In spring a tornado comes.
In spring the ice cream man faints.
In spring everybody turns into stamps.
In the spring rotten birds fly for air.

Henry Ponce

In spring the flowers get ugly.
In spring swimming pools get polluted.
In spring the beach is ugly.
In spring the United States gets like mud.
In spring the schools get muddy because boys make it muddy
    by shooting mud.
In spring sometimes flowers turn into money.

Cecil Santiago

In spring I play
I eat in spring
I do my work in spring
I'm good in spring
I'm doing things in spring
Spring, Spring, you're mine
Spring is the color of a rose
If I was spring
Spring, Spring, I'm calling you
Spring, Spring, play with me
Spring, Spring, I love you.

Maria Mesen

How Spring Got Its Name

PART I. Once there was a boy named April. Now it was warm weather out and the townspeople were trying to figure out a name for the weather. One day April walked over to a "spring" and he died! ! ! ! The headlines in the newspapers were

"APRIL INTO SPRING"

The townspeople loved him so much they called the weather

"SPRING"

PART II. And every "APRIL" "SPRING" comes along to say good-bye to winter and say

HI

to   all   his   friends.

Marion Mackles

Spring

Spring is like someone peeking in your window.
Spring is like waiting an hour for a green light.
Spring is like someone drawing a picture of a flower.
Spring is like falling off a chair.
Spring is like looking out of a window and falling down.
Spring is when you drop something and when you reach down
    to pick it up your pants split open.

Billy Constant

Spring

Spring what is spring?
Spring is an old thing like burnt toast I throw away
Spring spring where'd you go, now it's summer so hot.
Spring why did you go? We miss you.
Spring you're hot spring you're cold you're everything but
    springy.
You don't jump you shoot up you just stay here until you're
    ready to go.

Argentina Wilkinson

Once upon a time there was a very old woman who was walking down a road and had to rest and she saw a spring bed and sat on it and said "That's a good name, spring." So that is how it got its name.

Spring is like a green garden full of beautiful purple flowers in a field and spring is like a butterfly flying over the field, and it is like a ring in the sky.

Ruby Johnson

Comparisons Poem About Spring

Spring sunshine is like the shine of my desk.
Spring is like the day America became free.

Mercedes Mesen

Spring is like a ring in the sky
Spring is like a moon in the sky
Spring is like birds flying all over
Spring is like summer, but there's a difference,
Spring is like a spring of a mattress.
Spring is like jumping out of a seat
And last but not least
Spring is like nothing in the sky.

Ruben Marcilla

Comparisons of Spring

Spring is like a bowl of jello
shaking of the cold.
Spring is like a paper bag
(Always busting in the air).

Michael Carlton

Flyin' High

Spring is like a beetle coming out of its hole
Spring is like rolling on a damp lawn
Spring is a blue sky and blue as I dunno what
Spring is sailing a boat
Spring is a flower waking up in the morning
Spring is like a plate falling out of a closet for joy
Spring is like a spatter of grease
Flying high like Lucy in the sky
Spring is like doing a cartwheel on a sidewalk
Spring is like a bird flying over a lake
Spring is like putting on tennis shoes
Spring is like walking in flowers
Spring is like doing a bellyflop in a mudpuddle.

Jeff Morley

Spring is like. . . . a blade of especially sharp green grass
standing out from white, orange, and withery green
blades of grass.

Spring is like . . . sliding down a white hill and then, all of
a sudden, finding yourself rolling on green crayons.

Spring is like . . . washing yourself with white soap when all
of a sudden the soap turns green and brown and flower
designs appear on it.

Spring is like . . . when a cold day comes, suddenly a fire's
heat surrounds you.

Spring is like . . . cold snow in your hand while you are
building a snow fort when it immediately turns into
water and runs out of your grasp.

Spring is like . . . when your hands are freezing from lack of
gloves or mittens while you are playing with snow, all of
a sudden your hands thaw out and become warm.

Spring is like . . . being in a refrigerator and wishing to be
in a stove when suddenly you are in a stove!

Spring is like . . . bundling up in all your woolies, and
throwing them off when you get outside.

Lisa Jill Braun

Purpina's Spring

There once was a little purplish-grayish mouse.
Her name was Purpina and she had long fur.
She was walking in the woods on a nice day.
Purpina was thinking how the weather seemed to be getting
    warm.
Suddenly a clump of half-melted snow fell on her.
She was a little dazed. She couldn't get all the snow off
So Purpina sat down on a little hill.
Purpina soon fell asleep. When she woke up she got up.
Purpina tried to walk but she slipped and fell down the hill.
She was unconscious and when she woke up she found that
She was in a flower. She felt very warm and thought
She must name the kind of weather. First she thought
She would call it crocus because of the flower.
Purpina walked on and became very thirsty.
She came to a spring and drank a little water.
She was very grateful to the spring and told it
She would name the warm weather after it.
And that is how Spring got its name.

Erin Harold

If I Were the Snow, and Spring

The weather in its more dramatic forms is a marvelous stimulus to children's imaginations. My students wrote their Snow Poems during a snowstorm and Ron Padgett's students wrote their Spring Poems on a balmy spring day. The reality of the exciting weather outside affected their imaginations much as the works by Stravinsky and Mozart had when they wrote their Poems Written While Listening to Music.

One can help children find their freshest feelings about the weather by asking them to write about it from an unexpected point of view, as I did when I asked them not to describe the snow but to say how it would feel to *be* the snow. I reminded them that as snowflakes they could fall anywhere and could freeze people as well as make them happy. For the Spring Poem, Ron Padgett asked the children to say what spring was like (a specialized version of the Comparison Poem), and to say how spring got its name. If told merely to write a poem about spring or snow, children may get stuck in the conventional ways of describing them and not have the pleasure of creating something new.

Rainstorms, light spring showers, intensely hot or cold weather (you can open the windows for a while), and other meteorological events should furnish some fine occasions for poems in the course of the year.

Lies

Fourth Grade

Things That Aren't True

I was born in the blackboard.
I was a bear before I was born.
I was real big and then became little.
I was real then I was fake.
I was terrible then I was awful.
I was a fairy but they bit me and became ugly.
I became a plant then I became water.
I became America then I became London.
I became an eye then I became a nose.
I became an ear then I became a mouth.
I became a picture then I became a moon.
I became a thousand names like Ilona Elizabeth.
I became a doll then a giant.
I became a baby then a book.
I became a lion then a letter.

Mayra Morales

I am in New York in a cow's head.
I am still in New York in a cow's head.
I am still in New York in a cow's head.
Now I'm in New York in a flower.
I'm now in New York in a cow's head.
Now I'm in Spain taking a bath.
Now I'm in Spain taking a bath tub.
Now I'm in New England eating my friend in the bathroom.
Now I'm still in the bathroom eating my friend but I'm on a
     cow.
Now I'm in New York in a cow's head.

Marion Mackles

I am grass as green as can be.
I am in a tree on a leaf.
I am in New York on a flying blueberry.
Mud is pretty.
Rain is ugly.
I am on a vine.
I am snow.
I am snow in Spain.
I am rain in Spain.
I am the sun in Spain.
I am a cloud in Spain
I am in Spain
I am Spain

Marion Mackles

I was standing on the dirty street corner of Africa asleep eating a piece of lead. I was three hundred years old. The lead I was eating was orange. An orange walked up to me and asked me for a cigar. I didn't have one so I gave him a cigarette. He said thank you and politely walked away. I climbed up a tree where strawberries were growing. A strawberry looked at the lead I was eating and his blue hair stood up. I climbed down. I then walked over to a coconut bush. The coconuts were hungry so I gave them some cockroaches. They gobbled them up. Then I went back to my piece of skin and fell awake.

Eliza Bailey

I Was

I was in a cartoon on television. I was a broom standing in a
    corner. I swept floors with my feet. I didn't like sweeping
    floors.
I was bought from a store.
I was able to talk.
I was a movable broom.
I was very mad because all I did was sweep.
I was finally so mad I turned right back into a tree.
I threw my trees of oranges at the people I swept floors for.

Ilona Baburka

The Fruit School

I am a boy of bananas. I go to a school of apples. My teacher is made by oranges. My students are berries. The desks, they're cherries. The floors are whiskey and some are soda. The principal is a blackberry. The vice, blueberry. The library is redberry! My name is made out of grapes, my friends, it's a scrape. Know I am a boy, a plain own boy.

José Lopez

Fifth Grade

I live in the sun and am always freezing. My teacher is a monkey. My desk is made of roses and I have to water them every day. I go to school in a swimming pool. My spelling words are my name and address. I am a ball. I live under my books. I walk to the moon three times a week. I have muscles made of dew. When it is Christmas I go outside for Hallowe'en. My dress is made of wood. I read books about myself. I was going up to space in my father's car. I have hair made of eggs, dew, paper, meat, and cheese. My teeth are the moon, sun, earth and all the planets. Being in school at midnight, I can see the wind.

Mercedes Mesen

Sky Ship

I'm a boat that sails in the sky. I sail in the day go fishing
at night. I fish all night long and caught a flounder cloud it
was delicious to eat for a snack. My father's a steamship my
mother's a tugboat. Oh gracious here comes the moon he's
swooning at me see you later or he'll catch me, to eat.

Argentina Wilkinson

I fly to school at 12:00 midnight
I run to lunch at 9:00
I go underground to go home at 11:00
My name is Clownaround James Jumpingbean Diego Spin-
    around Jimmy and Flipflop Tom
My head was born in Saturn my arms were born in the moon
    my legs in Pluto and the rest of me was born on the earth
My friend the bee zoomed me home.

Eduardo Diaz

The Dawn of Me

I was born nowhere
And I live in a tree
I never leave my tree
It is very crowded
I am stacked up right against a bird
But I won't leave my tree
Everything is dark
No light!
I hear the bird sing
I wish I could sing
My eyes, they open
And all around my house
The Sea
Slowly I get down in the water
The cool blue water
Oh and the space
I laugh swim and cry for joy
This is my home
  For Ever.

Jeff Morley

Lies

I asked the children to put a lie in every line or else just to make up a whole poem in which nothing was true.

My students always took the word "lie" in the right spirit: I was asking them to make things up for a poem, not recommending dishonesty in their daily lives. Lying encourages very free imaginings. Often starting off saying untrue things as a joke, children become excited by the strangeness and beauty of what they are inventing.

Calling the poem "Lies" is better than calling it "Imaginary Things" or "Make Believe," words which have a built-in childishness and fairytale quality. Using them, children are more likely to write about dragons and gingerbread houses than about things close to them. "Things That Aren't True" is probably the next best way to put it. "Suppose" and "Pretend" are other possibilities; I don't like them much because they dictate a certain kind of wistful imagining. An exciting thing about invention is being caught up in it and starting to believe it; "Suppose" and "Pretend" keep saying it couldn't be true.

Lies are an exceptionally good theme for spoken collaboration poems. Sitting around in a group, the children are excited and inspired by each other's lies, and they try to top each other with statements stranger and more fantastic than the ones they've heard so far.

Colors

Third Grade

An apple is red.
A bird is red.
A funny old looking squirrel is red.
A pen is red.
A little red ball makes me feel happy.
A funny clown makes me happy because he dresses funny and
    his nose is red.
A suit is red as a tomato.
Red makes me happy because when a red umbrella flies up in
    the air.
Red makes me happy because when you take a bath you get
    wet.
Red is my favorite color because it is the color of the flag.

Carmen Berrios

Pink makes me happy
Red makes me sad
My luckiest colors are silver and gold
Pink is like a pig's tail
Pink is my favorite color
No matter if it's with a different color.
Pink is a beautiful color.
Pink is like a book of the school building
Pink is the color of my summer dress
Pink is like a summer flower.

Andrea Dockery

I like blue like a Pan
Am sign. It looks like a blue
Rainbow. Also looks like a blue
Sky and a blue sea and a blue
Coat and a blue tie and a blue
Jacket. And a blue jet.
And it looks like the New York
Jets uniform. It looks like
A flannel board and a blue rose
And a blue city full of blue
Houses and blue blackboards
And blue dirt and blue people.

Andrew Norden

I think red is as red as when the day is going away
I think red is when someone has died and gone forever
I think red is like a volcano blowing itself apart and leading
    its way to a deserted village
I think red is a sad way of saying death has arrived to do its
    evil deed
I think red is like the devil in its underground cave seeing
    evil things to do and destroy.

Chip Wareing

A horse is as brown as a pony
Wood was brown when I painted it
Give me some brown paper or I'll sock you in the pants.

Author unknown

Black makes me think of King Kong in my bathroom
Black makes me think of the dark.
It makes me think of the funny elephant that is black.

Lori Vasquez

Green

Green is the color of chalk.
Green is grass.
Green is the color of a shirt.
Green is peas.
Green is the color of a Christmas tree.
One night I was walking down a street. Then suddenly I
    turned green. Then the street turned green.
When I walked down the next block that turned green too.

Virginia Dix

Orange

Orange is a color of a pumpkin.
Orange is a color of an orange.
Orange is a color of a dress, too.
Orange is a color of nailpolish.
Orange is a color of a book.
Orange is a color of a crayon.
Orange is a color of a flower.

Zaida Rivera

My Dream of Africa

There are pink elephants because they are happy, so happy
    that they can fly.
Blue elephants can't fly because they are unhappy.
All baby elephants are green because they are growing.
And raspberries grow on daisy trees.
My Africa is the happiest place because it has lots of bright
    colors.

Vivien Tuft

Colors

My hair is redsilver
My eyes are greensilver
My teeth are bluesilver
My body is orangesilver
My skin is graysilver.

Lisa Smalley

My Favorite Color

My favorite color is orange. Everything is orange. Trees are orange, birds are orange, snow is orange, grass, you, me and goats, rain, sky and many more things. I like orange because it is a light color. Orange is like a melody singing by. Orange reminds me of floating in air. That's why orange is my favorite color.

Mayra Morales

The Most Beautiful Color Gold

I dream of a beautiful color and it is gold. Gold is my second favorite color. I think about the color gold every day and every time. I think you should think and dream about the color gold, don't you?

Madelyn Mattei

Pink is Mine

Pink is my color. I like pink because it is bright. When I think of it it makes me think of a pink sky, an Easter Bunny, a dress, a baby in a crib and it makes me think of myself.

Lorraine Fedison

Colors Are a Feeling

Red makes me feel like sunshine shining on a hill.
Blue doesn't look like red. Blue makes the day seem dull.
Pink doesn't make me feel like sunshine.
Pink unlike red makes me feel floaty.
Yellow unlike red makes everything around me sparkle.
Black makes me feel heavy, very much unlike red.
Green makes me feel like I'm all wrinkled up.
Green is not as pretty as red, pink or orange.
White makes me feel happy just as I am now.
Purple is the end of the day and my poem.

Eliza Bailey

Red

Red is the sun setting at night.
Red is the color of love.
Red is the color of a cherry.
Red is the color of an apple.
Red is the color of a kind person.
Red is the color of sweetness.
Red is the sun rising.

       Marion Mackles

Hula La-la and Colors

My teacher's name is Hula La-la
She is black and green.
She goes on purple trains.
She lives in a blue house.
She writes blue homework.

       Stephen Sebbane

Fifth Grade

The Happy Blue Day

It was time to get up when I opened my eyes my whole room
   was blue.
What could I do, everything was blue.
I went to the barn while I was running the sun was blue when
   I reached the barn the chickens were blue, the cows,
   horses, pigs were blue.
I went to eat my eggs were blue, my bacon was blue, even my
   milk was blue.
When the day ended something happened. A big colorful rainbow went across the room and everything turned back to
   the way it was.

Eduardo Diaz

Yellow

   Yellow, yellow, yellow. The sky is yellow. The streets are
yellow. It must be a yellow day. Everyone is yellow today. My
mother is yellow. My teacher's dress is yellow. But yellow
everyways.

Yellow, Yellow
Yellow

Elizabeth Cabán

Sky Blue Everything Blue

The sky was very blue one night it was a midnight blue.
I looked up and saw a blue moon, blue stars.
I was chasing a blue, green cat and a blue, red dog.
I saw a friend, she was blue too!
Everyone was blue, my house was blue, every house was blue.
My bed was blue and I was blue.
My mother was blue, my father was blue too.
Even my hamster was blue.
Everything was blue, the furniture was blue, even the T.V.
    was blue, too. It was a very blue place.

Argentina Wilkinson

Green

What's the matter with green today?
I like green in every way.
Why can I say go away green, what's the matter with green
    today?
Green why can I hate green today?
What's the matter with green today? Go away green!

Author unknown

Gold

My eyes are redly gold.
My cheeks are bluely gold.
My neck is greenly gold.
My knees are silvery gold.
My hands are brownly gold.
My arms are yellow gold.
My legs are orangely gold.
My feet are aqua gold.
My hair is whitely gold.
And my heart is truly gold.
    Is yours?

> *Lisa Jill Braun*

My Color White

White is as white as the snow,
As white as my teeth, my
dress is white and my
socks and shoes. White is a happy
color and a bright color.
I have a white purse and it
is shiny white.

> *Ruby Johnson*

What Shall I Chartreuse

Oh green, yellow, orange, pink, red, black, brown,
What shall I chartreuse today?
I could chartreuse with brown and gold,
Or I could red John in the nose. What could I chartreuse?
I put a green croak in Pinky's bed, what shall I chartreuse?
I could put a silver yeow on teacher's chair
What shall I chartreuse?
I could ooze the blue toothpaste in Dad's face. What shall I
    chartreuse?
What could I chartreuse if I got a paint brush?
Oh, oh I just wasted the day on thinking on what I shall
    chartreuse
But I could always think of something to crown yellow
    tomorrow.

Charles Conroy

Eight Trillion Green Years Away

Green is the color of the universe.
A steeple of stars all green
Towers over the world
The stars look like emeralds
Scattered through the greenish hue
Of the universe so green.
On a dark green planet
Eight trillion green years away
A frog sits in the green night
All you can see is a shimmer of green
On the skin of green algae
In that green planet
Eight trillion green years away
Through endless miles of green void.
Galorp, galorp, burble, gurble
The frog disappears in the dark green night.
In that green world an animal lives on green oranges
He wanders through the green endlessness of the universe.
Through the emerald green spire
To that small green planet
Eight trillion green years away.

Jeff Morley

I Had a Dream About Colors, All Kinds of Colors

One day I had a dream, it was about colors. I dreamed that I was in another world and was in colors. I dreamed that I was in color, all kinds of colors. I was blue, white, red, and green. I was like a walking rainbow, and then I woke in the dream, I was going to school and when I went into school the school was yellow with black polkadots. It looked beautiful and bright, then when I went into my classroom the classroom was all different kinds of colors. They were in stripes, squares, and all kinds of shapes. Then I did something wrong and the teacher scolded me and then she started turning green, purple, and all kinds of colors. Then at the moment we were going it went off. I woke up.

Zoraida Gonzalez

Blue

If I could change the world I would turn it blue. The sky would be blue along with the clouds, stars and moon. I would change whatever I could to blue. The houses and stores would all be blue and when the streets and all are fresh, next would be you!!

Mary Minns

Our Black and Blue Sun

If our sun was black and blue what color would you be?
Our buildings red, our face blue and our body black if you
     were walking upside down or running on your head I'll
     just jump down and kill myself and think you will do too.
Black black black blue blue blue bow wow boohoo hoo.

Carmen Velez

My Color Poem

If the water in the park was pink I will float and float until
     the little pink sun comes and dries me up.
I like pink because it's so bright and it makes me cry—ba, ba,
     ba, sob and for once and for all get me out of black.
I wish the clothes of Mr. Koch were pink and real pink and
     Mrs. Weick never uses pink clothes only red, blue, black,
     white and other colors but never pink only her nail polish
     is the only pink thing she has on pink. In other days she
     has orange, white and yellow or green sometimes.
        PINK IS MY COLOR! Sob!

Concepcion Dipini

Army Life

Captain Green was walking one day
Waiting and waiting for payday
Along came Captain Scarlet and bopped him on the nose
Sergeant Green came and zapped him in the eye "Zap"
Then came Captain Marvel of Whiz Comics
Then came the battle of four armies
Bombers dropping purple bombs and scarlet bombs
Green Sopwith Camels charged.
Blue Spads, orange Fokkers, green Cockroaches
And 1,000,000 other kinds.
A green tomato charged
So did a pickle
I was so scared
I called Thor Okenshield
Soon Paris peace talks broke it up
And everyone went home.

Jean Morrison

Colors

Children love to write about colors, and colors had already appeared in many of their poems before I made this assignment. For these poems I asked them to put colors in every line —the same color or different ones. By devoting a whole poem to colors, they could concentrate on such pleasant things as the colors of sounds, words, countries, and numbers. They could also make one-color poems (like Picasso's blue paintings)— everything in the poem the same color or different shades of the same color. I especially encouraged them to try that. In presenting the theme, I did things to help them associate colors freely with everything else. I asked them to look at the sky and see if it was the color of anything in the room. I asked them to close their eyes, then dropped a bunch of keys on the desk and asked them what color that sound was. I hit the desk with a ruler and asked the same thing. I asked them to write down the colors of France, England, and Spain; of Monday, Wednesday, and the number fourteen hundred.

The idea for this poem came not only from the children's obvious liking for colors but also from a certain art and poetry display on the fourth-grade hall bulletin board. Here, amidst beautiful painting and silverfoil collage by fourth graders, were six sheets of notebook paper, each bearing the same poem, copied out neatly by different children. This adult's poem, apparently suggested by Walter de la Mare's "Silver," included the same color, silver, in every line. The message was that children could create original art but not original poetry. I decided to show how untrue this was by having my students write poems of the same kind.

Sestinas

Fourth Grade

The Problem of a Mystery

There is a mystery
House near the Mississippi
You are a fish
You live in the ocean
Your father doesn't have transportation
King Kong the beast

You are a beast
I saw a movie about a mystery
I don't like any transportation
I was born in Mississippi
I saw an ocean
I lived in a fish.

Our school is inside a fish
A flag is a beast
I live in the ocean
I saw a mystery
I love Mississippi
A fish went to get transportation

Your glasses are made of transportation
I saw a catfish
My father is Mississippi
When I get mad I'm like a beast
This world is a mystery
I saw a blue ocean

That is a quiet ocean
There is no means of transportation
I saw a stupid mystery
I saw a flying fish
I sat on a beast
I live with Mississippi

I wish I was Mississippi
There is an atomic ocean
I killed a beast
I can't find any transportation
What is a fish
A fish is like a mystery

You are a mystery and Mississippi
I am a fish swimming in the ocean
I was looking for transportation but I am a beast.

Mrs. Magnani's Class

Fifth Grade

Hooray

My wonderful perplexity
Is so disjoint.
Words like that are not common
But they do have quite a wealth
Of meaning. Hooray! Hooray!
It's really fabulous.

It's a wonderful fabulous
Day! Let's have some perplexity.
It's time we got some hooray!
I think I'll just disjoint
Altogether. Look who's here! the wealth
Man! His visits aren't so common.

Today isn't so common
But tomorrow will be fabulous.
We want wealth
But getting wealth is a great perplexity.
I've got a disjoint.
My finger fell—hooray!

It's time for lunch hooray
What do work and lunch have in common?
I'll go have something to eat in a disjoint
Restaurant. The food there was fabulous!
Food is a great perplexity.
Food is great wealth.

Here comes the Wealth
Parade! No one is going to say hooray.
Why that is is a great perplexity.
A parade isn't common
But it's fabulous.
The wealth man's float is going to disjoint!

Things like that are disjoint.
How should we distribute the wealth?
Distributing wealth is fabulous.
They're distributing wealth—hooray!
Distributing is so common
We'll distribute it with the perplexity.

The perplexity of the cat is disjoint.
It comes out in common with the wealth
Man. The people will say, "Hooray! it's fabulous!"

Mrs. Weick's Class

Barp

Grass is always pink
Lucy's face is aquamarine
But from a distance it looks green
Let's have some jazz that's blue
Wouldn't you like your jazz purple
Instead? Lucy's hair is red.

Roses are red
Violets are pink
Sugar is purple
Your nose is aquamarine
Her teeth are blue
Her eyes are green

All this sickening talk is turning me green
She stayed in bed all day with red
I like your tie, your tie is blue
It has polkadots pinker than pink
He is the son of the aquamarine
Let's end the verse with purple.

When will the sky turn purple?
And when will the sun turn green?
Today the sun and the sky are aquamarine
Charlie Brown was brown, but now he's red
And Snoopy's nose is very pink
I wish the world would turn blue.

Here comes the furious Captain Blue
And right behind him is Mr. Purple
But now here comes the lady in pink
And Mr. and Mrs. Green
There goes the stupid knight in red
And they all say Goodbye aquamarine

We just found out the stars are aquamarine
And we also found out that the moon is blue
That the planet Mårs is red
And also that space is purple
And here comes Galileo dressed in green
With his telescope painted in pink.

"Let me sleep with pink on checks that are aquamarine"
He thought space was green and the planets were blue
And that the earth would soon be purple and red.

Mrs. Weick's Class

Sestinas

The sestina was invented by the troubadour poet Arnaut Daniel. Dante wrote one, and there are sestinas in English by Spenser, Sidney, Rudyard Kipling, Ezra Pound, and W. H. Auden. It is a complicated poetic form which can be made easy for children to write. Children enjoy the game and puzzle aspect of this form, in which lines have to be made up to fit certain words which appear in a predetermined order at the ends of the lines. Finding these lines excites their imaginations, and in making up sestinas they learn something about repeating words in different contexts which they can enjoy using in other poems.

The simplest way to understand the sestina is to look at one the children wrote. In "Barp," for example, the end words are all colors: pink, aquamarine, green, blue, purple, red. For the first 36 lines they recur in a certain order: 123456, 615243, 364125, 532614, 451362, 246531. In each of the last three lines there are two end-words, and the order is 123456.

To make things easier I had the class compose the sestina together. I explained the form, then asked for suggestions for the six end-words. If most of the class approved of a word suggested, I wrote it down. After we had six, I made a sort of skeleton of the poem on the blackboard. All 39 lines were there, blank except for the end-words, which were printed at the end of the lines in proper order. For "Barp," what I put on the blackboard looked like this:

————————————— pink
————————————— aquamarine
————————————— green
————————————— blue

_____ purple
_____ red

_____ red
_____ pink, and so on.

I asked for lines to fit the end-words, starting with the first, of
course, and on to the end. Children raised their hands and
offered lines. If it fitted in with the end-word and if the other
students approved, the suggested line would be printed on the
board as a part of the poem. As in other spoken Collaboration
Poems, the children inspired each other. Six or seven especially
articulate children had the most to say, but by various kinds
of encouragement I was able to get others to take part.

The children enjoyed writing sestinas. Other complicated
forms can be made available to them too, or a teacher can
invent forms in which certain words are given beforehand and
the rest is left for children to fill in.

Poems Written While Listening to Music

Fourth Grade

The Music

The music makes me think of dancing in a big room full of dreams and excitement and the loud music makes me think of the Egyptian times when there is a boat and the boat is rocking and rocking and the boat turns over and everyone falls in the water and they never come back because they turned into fish and they can't turn back into people. And it makes me think of a Spanish dance in the times of the pink lace dresses and the King comes and he comes with soldiers and comes to take the princess away.

Ilona Baburka

The Beautiful Day in Spain

I was looking at the sun and I saw a lady dancing and I saw myself and I kept looking at the sun then it was getting to be night time then the moon was coming up and I kept looking at it it was so beautiful that I couldn't take my eyes off of it. It was the sun and the moon that were so beautiful.

Ileana Mesen

Mr. Koch and the Color White Go

This music sounds like Mr. Koch dancing on air and he is very nice he tries to warn me that somebody is going to hypnotize me but I do not listen so there goes the color white with Mr. Koch. The music of the violin makes me feel like I'm going to another dimension.

Madelyn Mattei

It makes me think of the Ice Capades when it is dark and a man and a lady were on the ice and they were spinning and spinning and they never stopped.

Maria Ippolito

Flowers and the Center

I was walking through a garden at Queen Elizabeth's palace. As I walked through, the flowers nodded their heads and did little dance steps. Then Queen Elizabeth invited me into her palace. She gave me a silken robe and the roses danced behind me holding up my train and nodding their heads. Then it all turned dark and I woke up. I was very sleepy.

Eliza Bailey

The Gardens of Spain

In Spain I hear lots of beautiful records. When I hear them I feel like I am floating in the air and it also feels so romantic and I also feel that I am falling apart while I am floating in the air. I am throwing roses and when the records stop I stop. I feel like I am jumping off the roof, everything is over, I'm falling.

Lisa Smalley

Beautiful music feels to me like you have no problems just floating on air looking at the beauty of the Earth see all the different countries. Sometimes music makes me feel kind of sad too. I feel like I'm a bird flying over the Grand Canyon.

Stephen Sebbane

Yay No Homework

This record makes me feel like all the children in Mrs. Strasser's class all going home very happy because there isn't any homework. The ones that are very happy are Steven, Tommy K. and me. All the children are playing and laughing because Mrs. Strasser is on a deserted island climbing date trees for food. The children hope that she stays marooned on the island forever.

Thomas Rogaski

Help

The world is coming to an end. I am falling in a deep hole deeper deeper deeper deeper. My father is driving a car suddenly something white is in the air we are being taken in a new dimension strange sounds I am yelling suddenly I am alone I see all different colors I am falling in a rainbow my brain is getting mixed up I am seeing things no! I am not seeing things! People made of glass you can see through them! they look like fire in ice. Help!

Tracy Roberts

A Spring Day

The song reminds me of children walking through the garden in Spain. It is sunny and gay. They're going to the mountain and they are sitting. Then they fall down. It is dawn. They go home. They go running. Now the children stop, they are tired. They go to sleep. Then morning comes, they are lost. The two children want to go home. A strange monster comes and grabs them. The monster becomes their friend. He feels sad. But the monster will return. Then they find they're in China. They go wandering through the garden. They are home. They are glad. Then they go to sleep and they'll always stay home.

Mayra Morales

The Sounds

The rocket landed on the moon. And the moon men are walking and they hear these strange noises and the creatures come and come closer to the moon men ready to attack and they all come out of their underground houses and attack the moon men. The moon men are using all their equipment to shoot and kill the monsters of the unknown planet. And the leader of all the monsters yells out to the monsters and says Kill Kill KILLLLLL. And the moon men take an explosive and blow up the whole planet into big horn stars that blow sounds from the horn.

Ilona Baburka

Fifth Grade

Blahhh

Tweet, twang, twoot
Tweet, tweet, blaah, tweet, tweet, blaah
Twinkle, twixt, twang, la, la, la, la
Swung, sweurt, sleep, sleep, sleep
Blah, twang, sweurt, twoot, tweet,
Tweet, tweet, tweet, blaahh
Honk, tweet, twang, blaahh
Wwwaaaww, winky, dinky, doo,
Stunky, dunky, dee, dee, doo, dum
Tweetle, tweetle, twack, tweet, twunk
Braap, braap, twing, twung, sleeeep
Brap, sleep, brap, sleep, slurp, slap
Slumpy, dumpy, tweetle, dee, twink
Wank, twink, twank, blah
Pink, plank, plunk, ploo
Ponkey, bonkey, lonkey, loo
Sleep, blah, sleep, blah
Blahhhhhh!
Pinka, plinka, plank, plank, plunk, plunk.

Charles Conroy

Gardentail

Gardenia's walking over Nellie
And Gardenia is a mouse
Her tail's still over Nellie
Who would rather step on tail
Gardenia's walking through the grass
But her tail is still on Nellie
Gardenia's going uphill
Gardenia's going downhill
She's wading through a stream
And her tail is off of Nellie
Nellie's running after
But she's slow as a snail
Gardenia's tail's all in the grass now
But Nellie's stepped on top of it
Poor Gardenia can't go now
Nellie calls her Gardentail
And says tail grows on her
Gardentail is free now
And happy happy happy
Her tail follows her up
And also down
But a long time after she was there
Her tail goes over molehills
And around pebbles
And up down up
And all up or down
And Nellie can't catch up.

Erin Harold

In the Park

We were dancing and laughing when we saw a little bird, he came into my hand and said, "Can I dance too?" Now we were dancing with a bird. Then came a little boy, very sad and said, "Can I dance too?" Now we were dancing with a boy and a bird. Everybody disappeared we were left alone. The earth opened, we were in danger, we held hands and cried, nobody came we fell in the earth, inside was a beautiful girl dressed in white. We went to touch her and she was air. Then we heard a girl cry, we looked but nobody was there. We walked and walked, we came to a great hole where there were many fruits. We dropped into the hole. It had nothing. Before we knew it we were back to the park with many children playing and old people feeding the animals. The hole was the chimney of our home. Our mother was happy to see us again.

Mercedes Mesen

The Mix-up Music

It sounds like a person with pink roses on them
It looks like someone crying
The color looks like blue, green, black
It sounds like it was taking place in a music room, in outer
      space with no one there like on Mars
It sounds like if someone was going to jump off the roof saying
      good-bye
It's like a cat and a rat playing tic-tac-toe three in a row
It's just things mixed together
It's like if someone was saying come with me I want you to
      come with me
It's like no one in the house
A pig and a mouse playing
A cat and a dog kissing, saying I love you.

Maria Teresa Rivera

A Landslide

There was a landslide in Alaska
It was coming down very fast to the village below
It fell on top of my friends
It fell on top of me
It broke down the village
After it stopped all was quiet
I came out
Then all of a sudden from nowhere the
    Abominable Snowman came
Everybody started running and it was really a snowman
I looked around and nobody was there,
I started calling and calling
Nobody came out and I was lonely
Because everybody left me
I sat on a snowrock
Then out of nowhere came company
It had something like a black mask
And it was black and white
It's a raccoon
I was so glad that I don't know what I did.

Ruben Luyando

I'm Only for Brown

When the sun goes down
In my mind the sky is brown
In your mind maybe yellow, red or pink
But all those colors are just for a fink
Pink is for the end of life
But brown you can look at all night.
The reason I don't like red
Is because girls like red
And I can't stand girls
With their head full of curls.
I'd rather eat a brown crayon
Or suck a lollipop made of rayon
Rain is brown when it hits
The ground in my mind
MY HEART IS DYING FOR BROWN

Music, only music is so lovely
That makes my feet go
Above me. Music is the
Beginning of life.

What a lovely mind I have!

Michael Carlton

Dancing Down the Stream

Violins play for me as I dance down the deep blue stream
I dance on my white toes as I dance down the deep blue stream
Flowers fall on me as I dance down the deep blue stream
Soft white snowflakes fall on me as I dance down the deep blue
    stream.

Lenora Calanni

The Dancing Ballerina

When the shiny ballerina dancer dances in joy and gallops through the bright stage why the audience applauds. Then she'll stand on her tender toes, she'll dance between the shiny crystal stage. Once more the dancing ballerina will sweep in happiness and will once again dance.

Luis Scifo

The Man and the Flute (Tweet Too!)

A little man with a flute in his mouth
He is walking through the forest.
And rabbits, cats, dogs, birds, monkeys, etc., are behind him.
Once he blows his flute five times.
Tweet tweet sings the singing bird.
The little man comes to a country
With his animals behind him.
They all sit down on the grass.
But they all are still singing and tweeting.
And the rabbit is still trying to catch up.
And when the man blows his flute
Very quickly the rabbit catches up.
And they get off the grass and meet some ballet dancers.
The ballet dancers dance, and sing very sweetly
And everything flows away ready for another day.
Now it is time to wake up.
The animals are still singing and squeaking.
But very sweet squeaking sounds.
They all are saying and singing
Tweet, tah, twoo, tak, teek.
And singing ti ti ti ti ti.
And singing ta ta ta ta ta.
And they all get tired and go
To sleep. Good song.

Tomas Torres

A Good Day's Journey

I set out on my journey to a town far away
My faithful cat Crumps is behind me
We pass along a beautiful trail
A bluebird chirps and a turkey struts away
I meet a badger and he tells me to play my flute
So I do and our merry group continues
Oh, oh I'm so tired, cries Mr. Badger
Let us rest, I said when I sat down the ground was soft and
cool
But then Crumps and I went down to the stream, and the
water was deliciously cold
The flute sounds beautiful
The day is overcast but beautiful
Suddenly a
Ooo boo hoo wah
What's that?
Mr. Badger returns with a bird who is hurt
But he recovers and likes my flute
The bird who told me his name was Whimpy rides on my
shoulder
And we gaily continue on
We stop and examine some nature things
Ahead I think I see the village
Yes, and we continue down the rocky mountain trail
We reach the village
And I hand my dear grandmother the good hot bread
It is late and the blazing orange sun drops behind the end of
the earth
I snuggle into bed and dear Crumps curls up on the floor
The stars twinkle and shine
I slowly drop off to sleep.

Jeff Morley

Sixth Grade

As I walk through the water, a new world appears before me.
A world of colors, red, yellow, green and orange.
This whole world appears before me.
I wish to soar like a bird in the yellow-green sky,
I wish to fly.
I wish to swim, like a tiger-striped fish,
Through blue waters and coral gardens.
I wish to run, like a swift and graceful impala,
Oh, my dreams, oh, my wishes.
Oh, to swim like a fish, in water.
Oh, to run like an impala through woods.
Oh, to fly like a bird through a wonderful sky,
But alas, I am naught but I.

Ruben Marcilla

A Black Night

It was pure black outside
Out of nowhere came out a burglar
He shot me and I fell dead
He ran and ran
I had a funeral
Everyone was quiet

Joseph Peck

The Snow

I woke up one morning and it was snowing on my farm.
There was snow all over on the house, on the road.
There was snow everywhere on my cow, on the pigs too.
I jumped to my feet and played in the snow.
I talked to the pigs and the cows
They told me they liked it I said, I do too.

Author unknown

A wave is rolling in the ocean.
A storm is coming
And it finds itself roaring high above the beach.
Suddenly it's all over and
Part of it is just a pond
Farther up on the beach where the rest of the water can't
    reach it.
Now a big flock of birds come.
It begins to rain and it grows bigger and bigger.
Something streaks by to the ocean.
And it begins to swim and swim and suddenly it disappears.

Robin Harold

I Now Pronounce You Man and Wife

Hold your hands together
Do you take this man as your husband?
I do.
Do you take this woman as your wife?
I do.
I now pronounce you man and wife.
You can kiss.
Do a dance called an uncle of the groom.
Soon everyone was dancing.

Joel London

The end of a sad story
Someone who was lost at sea and just lost
His chance to be rescued
Someone tiptoeing on the sidewalk
Someone who has lost his best friend
Someone who is gloomy
Someone running away on a horse.
Like a Mexican woman dancing
Ballerina dancing.

Author unknown

I see a lonely girl riding a horse along a lonely beach.

With the salt air going through her blonde hair.

She is lonely because her boy friend has left her.

The girl keeps on riding faster and faster, as the waves come in.

She stops and gets off the horse and sits down on the beach.

The girl is staring into the clear blue sky, trying to forget her unhappy thoughts.

Then she begins to weep and weep for her thoughts are darkened.

Suddenly she takes the reins of her horse and walks away.

Debbie Novitsky

In the windows of stores talking
To the wind that is hitting it softly.
The wind got mad and started to blow harder.
The windows got very sad and wouldn't talk any more.
The next night the wind started to tell the window sorry
But the window still didn't talk.
The wind was very sad and never came back again to the store
    window.

Antoinette Greene

Out from the dark comes a loud bark
The rustling of leaves and squeaking of weeds
Out comes the dark to strike again
People running and all are stunning.
The dark is a very nice place
But it is scary
I think the color is black
In the daytime the dark breaks
And out comes the beautiful day.

Angel Torres

Poem

The sky was closing in
A deep dark grey
The animals ran
To hide away
The wind was
Elegantly swaying the trees
Then it happened
Lightning crackled
Thunder roared
It rained
It rained
And rained some more
The animals slowly leaving
The trees drank to their hearts' delight
The remaining animals came out from hiding
And then it happened.
No more lightning
No more thunder
The rain . . . had stopped.

Amy Levy

Poems Written While Listening to Music

Music puts children in a dreamy, excited, creative mood, and they enjoy writing poems while listening to it. P.S. 61 had a phonograph for classroom use; I brought my own records. Different records, as one would expect, suggested different kinds of poems. The fourth graders listened to De Falla, Ravel, and, later, Varese; the fifth graders, to Stravinsky; the sixth graders, to Mozart.

To help make the music more inspiring to the writing of poetry I encouraged the children to make some associations of the music with sounds, colors, places, times of year, feelings of happiness and sadness. I asked them to close their eyes while I played a record for about a half a minute, then I asked them questions about it: Did you see a city or the country? Was it warm or cold? What colors were there? Then I put on a different record (I wanted it to come as a surprise) and asked them to write. I told them to write whatever the music made them think of—their poem could be a story, a dream, a description of a scene, whatever they wanted.

There will probably be more sense of form and richer content in the Music Poems if they are written after poems with a definite form (Wish Poems, I Used To / But Now) and poems with varied sensuous and thematic content (Comparisons, Noises, Colors, Lies, Dreams). If the children seem uncertain as to how to divide Music Poems into lines, one can ask them to listen to the music, write one line, then pause and listen for a moment again before writing the next one, and so on.

I used symphonic music, but many kinds of records would be good to try: rock, jazz, Indian music, flamenco, African drums, as well as recordings of birdcalls, railroad trains, the ocean, and other sounds of nature and of civilization.

I Seem To Be / But Really I Am

Fourth and Fifth Grades

My friends think I'm not equal
But I know I'm as good
My friends think that I'm not as smart as them
But I know I am.
Everybody thinks I hate cities
But I couldn't live on a farm
My parents think I hate my brother
But I couldn't do without him
Some think I can't run as fast or throw as far
But I know I can
Most people do not think I am an animal lover
But that is what has kept me up
My brother and sister don't think I will succeed
But I know I will.
Most people think if one of my friends is gone he's gone
But really my best friend saves me every time he talks.
Most people just think that I think the situation is bad
But I know it's horrible.
Many think I don't care
But really I want the world to be one family.

Jeff Morley

Another World

Am on the beach all alone I hear the waves so beautiful that it is the wind is blowing in my face I feel as though I were in another world where angels sing a lovely tune and flowers glisten when they do. I feel so light that I fly in the sky with wings that brighten all the sky and I feel so strange that I cannot see but one does not tell anything by their eyes one tells with the heart and with the mind.

Iris Torres

I Seem to Be But I Am a . . .

I seem to be a man in the flying trapeze. But I am a man in
the garbage can.
I seem to be an eagle taking a path of clouds. But I am a devil
taking baths of fire.
I seem to be a crocodile. But I'm a fish being stretched in a
whale.
I seem to be a man diving in the water. But I'm a gorilla
swinging from a tree.
I seem to be a pretty color. But I am a word that means gone,
that word is: The End.

José Lopez

My Only Lover Boy

When he was down in the yard
and when I was in the window
with my father and mother and
him with his mother and father too
and my mother was staring at
me and father said, "You ugly
and little thing what are you
looking at?" And I said, "At
my only and lover boy"
and father said, "What is
his name?" I said "His name
is Bobby Perez and I love him
a lot" and so I was twenty-three years old
when I got married with
my only and lover boy
and he was twenty-four, just a
year more than me.

Concepcion Dipini

My Little World

My little world is an empty
one. And sometimes I can
hear a sound of an animal
walking toward me. The
next morning I thought it
was for real but I realize
it was a dream. But the
dream I had I cannot
forget. But a dream like
that I cannot forget.

Lucille Perez

Sixth Grade

People think I'm so and so
But I am not so and so
People think I'm this
But I am that.

Margarita Cuadrado

I seem to be shy when she passes by, but inside of me I have
    a wonderful feeling.
She has a kind face, one you like to step on.
As we went for a walk in the park I felt a wet kiss hit my dry
    skin.

Robert Siegel

When I am with my friends I am shy
I can't talk and oh my eyes they are almost closed
I try my best to make lots of friends
But I get all shaky and blow my nose
Then I try to back out
And when I do I run home and that's all I do.
When I listen to music
I sit in a chair
And I close my eyes
Such like a bear.
I start to dream a silly dream
That I am flying in the air
When the music stops I wake up with a sharp
Then I put another one on and start all over again.

Antoinette Greene

My Own Little World

We go to the beach
I look at the sea
My mother thinks I stare
My father thinks I want to go in the water.
But I have my own little world.
I stare,
I see myself
I walk along the beach
Not another soul
But me.
I walk to a white horse
Snowy is her name
I get on
I hold tight to her manes
I nudge her slightly
She walks,
The sun is setting
The sea is quiet
The sand is moist
The air is tender
The sky is all the colors of the rainbows
I kick her harder
My hair blows in the wind.
On to the destiny, of nothing
It seems endless
I think perhaps it is
My own little world.

Amy Levy

I seem to be nice and kind
But I am really kind of mean.
When I stop my friend while we are walking along the beach
He probably thinks my feet are hot.
But I really stopped to look at the girls in those new bathing
   suits.
When I stay up late my mother thinks I'm watching the news.
But I watch those fashion shows with some of the girls wear-
   ing those bathing suits which make the girls look half
   bare.

Michael Lenik

To my friends, when we play football, they think I can't play.
But really I know how to play football.
When I go out with my friends I act tough, but when I am at
   home doing nothing, I am not tough because there is
   nobody to be tough with.
When I play with my brother he has to always beat me up.
But when we don't play I always beat him up.
When I say I'm sick I don't have to wash the dishes.
But I'm not really sick.

Carmine Vinciforo

Me

They say I'm a chicken
But I'm really tough
They say my punches are weak
But they're really rough.
They say I'm going to be a midget
But I'm really going to be big
They say I cannot carry six pounds
But they don't know I could carry 100.
They say it takes a year for me to run a block
But it really takes me about five seconds.
They say I'm going to die at eighteen
But I think I'm going to die at forty-seven.
They say I never find money
But one day I found $25.15.

Miquel Lopez

Really

I seem to be so dumb to my teacher, it seems.
But he really doesn't know me, really.
To my mother I seem to be a brat, it seems to be.
But I really am kind and good, really.
I seem to be shy to some friends I know, I seem to be.
But really, I'm not shy, really.
To my cousins, I seem to be a baby, I seem to be,
But really, they don't know me too well, really.
To the students of the class I seem to be kind of dumb, I seem
    to be
But really, I'm kind of smart, really.
To other people I seem to be a stranger
But really, I'm their sister, really.

Gloria Peters

When I'm alone
I think of the one I met at the age of four.
I also think of the one that passes by as I shy away.
I think of the one that makes fun of me but I don't care. I
   like them all.
But when I'm with friends
I melt my thoughts of the three I love
I turn away from them
But when I'm alone again
I brush my hair and look in the mirror and there he stands,
   he never goes.
I smell the flowers set on the table and I smell the love
   between us.
I turn the lights off and go into bed and dream of the lovely
   things I wish.

Natalie De Stefano

I Seem To Be / But Really I Am

The subject is the difference between the way one seems to other people and the way one "really is"—that is, the way one feels deep down inside that one is. The contrast can take many forms. It can be about conscience: I seem to be good, but really I'm bad; about being misunderstood: I seem to be mean, but really I'm nice; about shyness; about lying. Among sixth graders hidden romantic feelings were a frequent theme.

I suggested a two-line repetitive form similar to the one in the Used To / But Now Poem: begin every odd line with "I seem to be" and every even line with "But really I am." Like other suggestions I made about form, it was only a suggestion and no one had to use it.

The subject is serious, for older children at any rate, and playful tricks such as those I used with the Noise, Color, and Comparison Poems aren't a help in getting children in the mood to write about it. What I wanted them to feel when they wrote was some of the strangeness and silence of their deep and private feelings about themselves. I read aloud some short poems by D. H. Lawrence—"Trees in the Garden," "Nothing to Save," and "The White Horse"—to help them get in touch with these feelings there in the classroom. With the sixth graders especially the Lawrence poems had a noticeable (and good) effect.

Being an Animal Or a Thing

Fourth Grade

Dog

Oh dog, how do you feel with so much hair around you?
Dear master, oh my dear master, I feel nice and warm.
Oh dog, how do you feel with those fluffy ears?
Dear master, oh dear master, I feel as if I had super hearing.
Oh dog, how do you feel standing on four legs?
Dear master, oh my dear master I feel light and strong.
Oh dog, I'll leave now. Goodbye.
Dear master, oh dear master I feel it, my heart breaking.

José Lopez

The guinea pig's eyes are as red as a heart. You run around and don't know where you're going. The strange feelings as you run around in your cage. Your ears so tender and light. That fur coat you wear it's so soft. You have fun and affection. I run around not knowing what's happening. It's like a world of your own.

Marion Mackles

Elephant

How does it feel to be an elephant?
You are very lucky, you don't go to school.
How does it feel?
They say you are very fat but if I was an elephant I would be
    very scared to walk the streets because they would want to
    kill me. But I am not an elephant.
How does it feel with those big feet you have?
How do you blow your nose with that trunk of yours?
How can you walk?
Do you fall and break the ground because you are so fat?
How do you live?
How do you keep yourself warm?
How is your family?
I must go now. Good-bye.

Patricia Fernandez

My Dog

Oh my goodness!
Queenie is my dog
A dog is very nice.

All Queenie does is sleep and eat
If I was a dog
I would dance around the floor.

I would dance on my mother's head
I call my dog a white mud-pie face
Because he's all white.

Lorraine Fedison

My Hamster

My hamster is very bad
All he does is chew on lettuce
And jumps out of his cage.

And I have to catch him with my bare hand
And he bites me
So I yell and I say cock-a-doodle-do.

Lorraine Fedison

The Butterfly

Where has my butterfly gone?
He is not in the meadow, not in the field.
Not in the park, not in the garden.
Oh, where has my butterfly gone?
But today I found him in my house.

Thomas Rogaski

Lizard

Where is the ugly lizard
That mean old grouchy lizard
That moves along like a clam
That eats nice little fishes
Oh, there he is. Goodbye.

Thomas Rogaski

I Wish I Was a Lion

I wish I was a lion because you grow fur around your neck
    and you always keep warm. What?
Ha, ha, ha it's so funny.
I'm not going to write this terrible poem over again so shut
    up and don't say another word about this poem.
I was to be a lion but the skin tore
But I fell on that dirty floor.

Fontessa Moore

Zebra

The zebra would try to keep warm in the cage.
The zebra would eat all kinds of meat.
She will keep his stripes black and white.
Because the rain smears the stripes
And when it rained she would paint his stripes on again.

Lisa Smalley

A Dog

A dog is mean in one way and silent in another. A dog has its
    own way of thinking.
A dog is very friendly to his master.
If I were a dog I'd feel like I came from another world because
    I look different from human people.
Oh dog, how do you feel
The way you look?

Ilona Baburka

What It Feels Like to Be a Mr. Koch

If I were a Mr. Koch I would feel tall and lumpy. I would
    get the flu once or twice. And then I get the one I love.
Lives! Of course it would be hard to give him this all of this
    in one day because I am a sickness green shirt he has on!
    Oh, and you know why he would be lumpy because he'd
    get small pox!
    THE SICK END!

Tracy Roberts

Questions to Ask Snow Person

1. Do you like to be what you are?
2. Do you like when people step on you and make snow balls with you?
3. Do you like your color white?
4. Do you like to be mixed with snow?
5. Do you like to stand all day out in the snow with nothing to do?
6. Do you like when people fall on you?

Snow
The answer is
NO! ! !

Jeannie Turner

A Blackboard

How does it feel to be a blackboard?
I think it would feel funny.
Always being written on.
Always having examples erased off.
What do you see?
You see many, many kids.

Rodney Wills

A Design

What does it feel like to be a design? I would feel all pretty and outstanding. It would be fun to be a design because you would be all different colors. You would also shine because it would look all matched colors.

Ilona Baburka

Two needles were talking.
One of them said tell me a story.
O.K. said the other one.
Well once two needles were talking.
One of them said how do you feel about going through material.
Well said the other I like going through satin and velvet but I can't stand going through that awful scratchy wool.
Yes, said the other one.
Oh that's not a good story! ! !
Well, then let's talk about something else.
Okay. Remember how they bent Mary?

Eliza Bailey

How Does it Feel?

Me: How does it feel to be a flower?
Flower: Well, how does it feel to be a person?
Me: Well, I feel good. I'm used to it.
Flower: I feel good. Because I'm so thirsty. That I open my
    root and I drink the water. Sometimes I am not thirsty.
    I have to put up an umbrella and I say It's raining, it's
    pouring, the old man is snoring.

Lorraine Fedison

I Would Feel

If I were a flag, I would feel like flag day
If I were a picture, I would feel like lots of things
If I were a tie I would feel handy
If I were a cow I would feel moos
If I were a hill I would feel rough
But I know I'm a boy
A plain old boy. And I like it.
Now, good-bye.

José Lopez

Window

If I was a window children would throw rocks at me. And the sun would shine at me and people open and close me.

Daniel Lacey

Me, a Book? You're Kidding

Thomas: Why are you a book?
Book: Because then everyone could read me.
Thomas: Why do you want people to read you?
Book: What's a book for?
Thomas: To read.
Book: Wouldn't you be a book?
Thomas: Yes, but what would I do?
Book: You would be smart, know hard words, have beautiful pictures in you and have any kind of story you want.
Thomas: How could I be a book?
Book: By just reading books and other things.
Thomas: Thanks for telling me that.
Book: Good-bye.
Thomas: Good-bye and thanks-again.

Thomas Rogaski

Mr. T.V.

Ho Mr. T.V. with a flick of my finger I see a movie or a
   colorful cartoon. I make you look funny.
Ho Mr. T.V. how does it feel to have an oil well in you?
Ho Mr. T.V. what is your favorite show?
Ho Mr. T.V. do you like mystery stories?
Or do you go looking at Chinese junks?
Do you owl at detective stories or at midnight do you show
   crisscross cars and go beepbeep?
Ho Mr. T.V. tell me in the big little voice of yours.

Thomas Kennedy

All Things

If I was a cloud I would feel wet
If I was a door I would feel hurt
If I was Guy Peters I'd kill myself
If I was a pocketbook I would feel heavy
If I was a light I would feel hot
If I was hair I would feel beautiful.

Lisa Smalley

How It Is to Be a Floor

I'm the floor of a house. Every time someone steps on me I laugh. But the people can't hear me. Whenever they step on my belly I really laugh hard. Sometimes when they step on my eye I get some dirt in it. But I love when they step on my back. When people step on my mouth I want to swallow them but I don't.

Billy Constant

The Sky

I feel like a blue piece of cloth with white dots with bugs flying all over me. It tickles. I don't really like it. All the people look at me and when I cry they embarrass me and call it stuff like rain and snow. I hate it.

Marion Mackles

A Pen

I would like to be a pen because every day I would dance and whenever I'm out of ink they would put me away until I got ink. And I would go any place people go.

Hector Figueroa

If I Was a Flag

If I was a flag
I would feel like April
With the colors red, white and blue,
I would feel happy flying like a bird,
Swing on air, with the breath of air.
I would feel pretty good standing on a pole with the people
      saluting at me.

Esther Garcia

Being an Animal or a Thing

Children feel close to animals and objects, close enough to talk to them, close enough to identify with them. Without much difficulty they can imagine what it feels like to be a dog, a fish, a teddy bear, a cloud, or a piano. This is one of the great fundamental poetic talents, and children have more of it than adults. They enjoy writing poems in which they can use it.

Not only is this kind of identification natural to children, it is also usually easier for them than description. They are likely to write more enthusiastically and more imaginatively from the inside than from the outside. In asking for poems about animals and things, I suggested they imagine they were the animal or thing and write from that point of view. A few examples in class are a good way to get them in a happy and identifying state of mind: How would it feel to be a TV set? I would have a big, blank face. Then there would be music and lights inside me. I didn't insist that the poems show complete identification with the object or animal; and in fact some are dialogues, some are written from the outside, some are half inside half outside. What I wanted, so the children would get the most from these poems, was that they feel for the subjects rather than merely observe them.

The Third Eye

Fourth Grade

The Third Eye

The third eye can see the angels in the sky.
The third eye can see Superman flying invisible.
The third eye can see God.
The third eye can see air in the room.
The third eye can see the cold in the air.
The third eye can see oxygen.
The third eye can see through cave-ins.

Madeline Rivera

My third eye can see heat.
My third eye can see spirits.
My third eye can see Jupiter.
My third eye can see Mars.
My third eye can see spirits' underwear.
My third eye can see wind.
My third eye can see breath.
Now it is time for my third eye to go to sleep.

Gladys Algarin

It can see God
It can see the wind
It can see the village
It can see me
It can see the sky
It can see my body
It can see my name
It can see my hair
It can see my coco
It can see my leg
It can see a bird
It can see a door
It can see you
It can see St. Bridget's Church

Rafael Soto

The third eye can see God
The third eye can see the Devil
The third eye can see inside me
The third eye can see the hosts
The third eye can see P.R.
The third eye can see my voice
The third eye can see my bones
The third eye can see the wind
The third eye can see the village

The third eye can see to Mars
My third eye can see God
My third eye can see the Devil
My third eye can see bones
My third eye can see breath

Robert Melendez

The third eye can see sound.
The third eye can see stars.
The third eye can see Superman.
The third eye sees inside of the paper.
The third eye can see inside of the clock.

Carmen Garay

The Third Eye

The third eye can see the wolf eat the three little pigs
The third eye can't see the wolf fall in blazing fire
The third eye can't see me eat up the cooks
The third eye can't see me do homework
The third eye can see the world
The third eye can see the house with the red room

Genett Way

Fifth Grade

The Eye Between My Eyes

Flick! a blue flashlight in front of my eyes. Oh God, that eye
    between my eyes.
Whoa horsey! My you're acting strange Mister Meridoe
    Brandy Buck. Oh God, that eye between my eyes.
Whoops I stepped off the earth and accidentally landed on it
    again. Oh God, that eye between my eyes.
Flash it's night already.
Flick it's day again. Oh that eye between my eyes.
    flash flick off you go
    flick flash on you go
Oh God, that eye between my eyes. You never stop do you the
    eye between my eyes.

Jean Morrison

The Third Eye

This is a magic power poem, like a poem about being invisible. Children are fascinated by physical transformations and added powers and like to write about them.

Ron Padgett asked the children to imagine they had a third eye in the middle of their foreheads and to say what it would see. The rule was that the third eye could see what the two regular eyes could not see and was only open when they were closed. It was exciting to think of all that one could not see, but knew about or could imagine, just as it was to think of wishes or lies.

To help the children enjoy this poem, the teacher should take the fantasy seriously and also perhaps indicate by a few examples the great variety of things we know about or think about but can't see and which thus the third eye might see: oneself as a baby, England, the middle of the Atlantic Ocean.

Except for "The Eye Between My Eyes," these poems are from Mrs. Magnani's fourth grade "N.E." class.

Collaborations by Two Students

Fourth Grade

False

The black sky shines in the morning!
No the green sun shines on my hair!
So I walk on the purple ground!
So my red lips shine on the plants!
So my pink shoes shine on my glasses!
So my brown coins shine on the garbage can!
So my yellow teeth shine on the water!
So my orange eyes shine on the desk!
So my green ring lights a fire!
So my blue fingernails shine on the blackboard!
So my gray notebook shines on your nose!
So my white blouse shines on my shoes!
So my red slip shines on the clock!
So my silver eyes shine on the ceiling!
So my violet car shines on the moon!
So my purple green dress shines in the sun!
So my silver red and black paper shines on the wall!
So my maroon body shines on the flag!

Jeannie Turner and Nancy Ortiz

Our minds, Vivien, are trying to be other minds.
People have red hair.
Birthday party for me, people can come to a special place.

Lorraine Fedison and Vivien Tuft

Imagination

The sky is blue green
Black for blackboard which stands there year after year.

Lorraine Fedison and Vivien Tuft

Imagination

With a circle going round within and without the moon and
    stars.
I wear a blue dress.

Lorraine Fedison and Vivien Tuft

Who was the first one born on Earth?
   Adam and Eve
Why was there such a thing as cavemen?
   They're just a figment of your imagination
What is the sun made of?
   FIRE!!!!!
Where did everyone get his birthday from?
   They voted on it
When was the moon discovered?
   100,000,000,000,000,000,000,000,000,000,000,000,000,000,
      000,000 years ago
How old is the Statue of Liberty?
   The same year as the moon was discovered.

Questions by Mayra Morales
Answers by Marion Mackles

What's inside the moon?
    There's hot water inside.
What's the sky made of?
    It was made out of white snow.
If you cut the sun open what would you see?
    Terrible looking enemies.
When you write you look at your words have you thought of
        cutting open a letter to see what's inside?
    No. But if a person was crazy the answer would be yes.
What's inside colors?
    There's pink stars.
Where is the end of the universe?
    In back of the swimming pools.
How old is adventure?
    It is 60,000 years old.
Which color is older, black or white?
    Black because you can outline me.

Questions by Vivien Tuft
Answers by Fontessa Moore

Collaborations by Two Students

Children like writing poems together, either in large groups or with just one other person. Some kinds of two-person collaborations have a particular charm for the chance they give to trick, tease, and outdo one's fellow poet, as well as to feel the immediate inspiration of his presence. It all happens more quickly, too, than in a group collaboration. One doesn't need to burst with ideas for so long; one can get them all out almost at once. The finished product has a kind of magic; written by two, often at cross purposes, amid excitement and jokes, it turns out to be one poem—interesting, beautiful, funny, and sometimes even making sense.

There are many kinds of Two-Student Collaborations. The ones here were written in three different ways: by two children sitting together writing alternate lines and watching the poem grow (Nancy and Jeannie's "False"); by two children sitting together writing alternate lines, with neither child seeing what the other wrote (Lorraine and Vivien's poems); by one child writing an answer to a series of questions proposed in advance by another (the poems by Mayra and Marion and by Vivien and Fontessa).

Nancy and Jeannie sat together and simply handed the sheet of paper they were writing on back and forth to each other. Lorraine and Vivien did the same, except that when one wrote a line she folded the paper over so the other couldn't see it. For the Question / Answer Collaborations, each child was asked to write a set of hard or even impossible questions on a sheet of paper. The papers were then collected and passed out at random. Children were encouraged to make their answers as strange as the questions.

Themes such as Colors, Noises, or Comparisons—in fact any of the themes used in this book—can be used in two-person collaborative poems. For example, Jeannie and Nancy followed Ron Padgett's suggestion and included a color in every line.

Collaborations can be part of regular poetry writing sessions too. Someone who has finished his poem can collaborate on a new one with someone who is stuck; and two who have finished their individual poems can go on to write a new work together. Theamondo Zaharias had trouble starting her Poem Using Spanish Words, so I suggested she do one in collaboration with Tomas Torres, who was sitting next to her and had already finished his. (Their poem is on page 293.)

Poems Using Spanish Words

Third and Fourth Grades

When estrella came the perro went to sleep.
And the manzana grew red, luna began to shine when the perro
    went to sleep.
And the felicidads in the house grew amarillo in a flowerpot.
The huevos thought the manzana was digging a hole.
And in the morning the cielo woke up and the España ate
    breakfast.
And the perro and the child went to Argentina.

Maria Gutierrez

The Guineo Was Tristeza in Argentina at Estrella

I wish I was a perro so I could crawl to my corazón and on my
    way I would slip on a guineo sky and fall on the luna.
I wish I was a manzana so when someone bit me I could bite
    back and they would land on an estrella.
I would be all these things and a caballo of someone's muerte
    would be cast over me.
I'd lose my corazón.

Markus Niebanck

A guineo is amarillo. When I eat them I think I'm a mono.
I am a niña, not a perro or a caballo.

Melissa Blitz

The luna is big and clara.
The perro I saw is almost as big as a caballo.
The caballo I saw ate the manzana I had.
The estrella was as clara as the sun.

Valerie Chassé

Fifth Grade

I saw a red and yellow vaca.
I saw a maestra with purple hair and green arms.
I saw a red and pink and blue cielo.
I saw a brown and green and gray muchacho in the casa.
I saw a fat muchacho with vaca hair.
I saw a vaca eating casa and flores and gato.
La vaca quiere el pato colorado el loco gusta el coco.
El coco her muerto in the casa.

Myra Garcia

I saw a yellow and blue cabeza!
I saw a man and woman amado in red.
I saw a marido in brown.
I saw a green cielo and a Cristo in red.
I saw a man loco in yellow.
I saw a loco man on a green toro.
I saw a big cabeza.
I saw a green and blue cabeza.
I saw a niña in gray.
I saw a ghost in navy blue.

Author unknown

I saw an amarillo perro.
I saw a Herman the monstro verde.
I saw a marido the una muchacha negro.
I saw an azul pelo.
I saw a blanca mano.
I saw a rosa flores.
I saw a colorada cara.
Yo quiero ver a Herman the monstro muerto.
Yo quiero ver a una muñeca bailando.
I saw a puerco comiendo.
I saw a conejo tocando piano.
Yo quiero ver a un cuchillo y un revolver matando.
I saw a pata de todos colores del mundo.

Linda Cruz

El mundo está bien requete loco y nosotros también.
Las niñas tienen el coco bien pelao.
El mundo va a esplotar mañana a las three.
El mar se va a secar y va a votar el agua.
Tan gente no se baña todos los dias.
La gente no van a poder comer.

Edwin Suárez

The Holiday

There was a special holiday called Carambano. It is in the verano. When Carambano comes, everyone eats their platos. The people's faces are rojo, azul, and amarillo. On this day people shoot estrellas. There is no sky over this planet. The planet is called Hombre.

Author unknown

Christmas on My Planet

On my planeta named Carambona La Paloma
We have a fiesta called Luna Estrella.
A funny looking hombre comes to our homes.
He has four heads: a león head, an oso head, a mono head,
    and a culebra head.
We do a baile named Mar of Nieve.
On this fiesta we eat platos.
That's how we celebrate Christmas on my planet.

Marion Mackles

Bomb-Bomb

In my ciudad in the primavera
There is a fiesta named Bomb-Bomb.
Down from the cielo come little amarillas estrellas.
And the árboles turn rojo and azul.
And the mar comes up on the costa.
On this fiesta we have cooked osa, boiled paloma, fried león,
    and for dessert we have carambano.
In the evening we sit around the mañana árboles and baile.

Jeannie Turner

Azul Christmas

In invierno there are carambanos.
In invierno they throw platos out in the nieve.
On Christmas there are bailes and beautiful estrellas in the
    sky.
On Christmas there is beautiful nieve.
On Christmas the colors people use are rojo and verde.

Lorraine Fedison

The León in Invierno

One invierno a león came to the nieve bosque.
And walked in the bosque and his garra was in the deep la
    paloma white nieve.
The trees had like white nieve plátos on the branch.
And it was Navidad la noche and the violeto cielo was full of
    baile estrellas.

Translation: *The Lion in Winter*

One winter a lion came to the snowy woods.
And walked in the woods, and his paw was in the deep dovey
    white snow.
The trees had like white snowy dishes on the branch.
And it was Christmas Night and the violet sky was full of
    dancing stars.

Ilona Baburka

Love in the Verano

My holiday is about love.
This holiday happens every day
All over the world.
The name of this holiday is Oso.
This is what happened to one couple
The girl's name was Rosa the boy's José.
He was a killer.
He had killed ten hombres and all the girlfriends he ever had.
Then he met a girl named Marion.
Her real name was Nina.
She came from another planet.
The planet Venus.
She had killed twenty hombres.
She loved him
He loved her
And that is love in the verano.

Tracy Roberts

The Holiday of the Azul Carambanos

I went to a beautiful land. I went to the land of the Azul Carambanos. It was beautiful. They celebrate a holiday. It is a wonderful holiday, it happens in the verano. This holiday lasts for three days. On the first day of the holiday people each eat azul carambanos. In the carambanos there is wisdom. The wisdom soaks into the people's heads, but if they eat more than one azul carambano, wisdom will seep out of their heads. On the second day of this holiday they ride caballos. Then they feed the caballos three azul carambanos each. Then the caballos have more wisdom than the humans on earth. On the third day of the holiday the people turn into beautiful people because of their kindness to the caballos. What is in the azul carambanos I can't tell you, for it is a secret.

Eliza Bailey

Galaxy Mono

That's rojo nieve outside it means that galaxy mono is coming to town yay! The holiday is invierno and the people are so happy. I hope I get a hot galaxy rocket to fly to the sky with my friend Billy and Stephen and we would bomb Lisa.

Guy Peters

Easter in the Under Ground World

Under ground there is a mar.
I live under the mar.
You'll see a big plato with little pieces of nieve.
We are celebrating a famous holiday now called Amarillo
    Leon.
During this holiday the cielo turns azul
The luna turns purpureo
The estrella turns verde
Also a manzana comes and gives us carambano.
That's how we celebrate Easter.

Marion Mackles

In invierno the sky is azul.
And in verano the cielo is light blue.
But what I like in invierno is that everybody pone pine
    arboles y they decorate them.
And in primavera flowers grow and leaves start falling off the
    arboles.
And in Puerto Rico la luna is amarilla.
And the estrellas are many colors.
And the grass is verde.

Esther Garcia

La Nieve

Un dia la nieve taba fresco la carambano taban frio yo taba temblado tel frio que me pusse amarilla. De la nieve salio una paloma y un mono me salio roja. El verano las estrellas bailon i gracies.

Mayra Morales

A Discovery of León in the Cielo

In the cielo you sometimes see a león.
The león means that that's a horoscope sign and every day you
    see the león in the cielo.
This holiday takes place on August 23, and on that day all the
    gente in the world come to Manhattan and get into a huge
    space ship and go up to the moon and they all have crayons
    and all follow the estrellas in the cielo and they draw
    their sign.
I hope my dream comes true because then I can go to the
    moon with an amarillo crayon and draw my sign in the
    cielo.
My sign is Libra and I would draw a scale in the cielo and
    then everyone takes an estrella as a silvernear.

Vivien Tuft

English & Spanish

I saw an hombre who had on an amarillo traje.
He put a culebra in the agua.
It was in the invierno time.
The culebra was verde.
Then suddenly it started to nieve.
Then the hombre started to do a baile.
Then he found a paloma close to muerte.
He was eating out of a plato.
This is what would happen to you on the holiday.

Fontessa Moore

Sixth Grade

I looked up to the cielo and it was amarillo and the luna was
    like manzanas and guineos.
Then the perro was tristeza and full of muerte.
After, Mickey el Ratón had felicidad in his corazón—he went
    to Argentina on a caballo.
I looked up to the sky and saw estrellas in the noche.
Then he went to España and said a palabra which was hello.

Tomas Torres and Theamondo Zaharias

The Yellow Heart
(El Corazón Amarillo)

I went to Argentina to get some bananas
Yo fuí a Argentina a buscarme guineos.
And I saw Mickey Mouse on my way.
Y via Mickey El Ratón cuando iba.
And he had a nose with an egg on it.
Y tenia una nariz con un huevo encima.
A dog came and bit his tail and he flew in the air.
Un perro vino y le mordió el rabo y brincó al aire.
Then I left and a horse kicked me.
Después me fuí y un caballo me dío una pata.
When I found my bananas, I bought an apple.
Cuando encontré los guineos, compré una manzana.
Then when I left on a plane, I found myself on the moon.
Después cuando me fuí en un avión, me encontré en la luna.
And there I stayed until my death.
Y ahí me encontré hasta mi muerte.

Ruben Luyando

When they told me I was going to España
My corazón turned amarillo
I was in the plane
I could see the estrellas
It was so triste
Those stars were all alone
But it was beautiful
Because the noche blended in with them
I started reading a book called Mickey el Ratón
After I got to España I went to a rodeo
I saw a lot of caballos
They were just in red and looked like a manzana
I looked up at the cielo
It was going to rain
I saw the perro eating a guineo
Then I went to Argentina
I knew there was going to be muerte
So I went home
When I got home I didn't say a palabra of what I had done
Anyway my heart was so red and sweet I named it a manzana.

Ivette Perez

My Noche Trips

I like to fly in the cielo at noche with a guineo
I do it every noche and say hello to the luna and the estrellas
Sometimes when I go up there I meet a caballo and a perro
When I am there the caballo and the perro are selling huevos
    and manzanas
I do this every night because I don't feel tristeza and it's
    felicidad to me.

Lenora Calanni

My Rockets into the Azul Space

I like to take rockets into the azul space.
I like to pay the luna a visit.
I also like to have tea with estrellas.
But most of all I like when the stars have felicidad parties at
    noche.

Lenora Calanni

The kaballah ate a noche and rode away on a caballo with a
    little corazón that was amarillo like guineo.
To Argentina he rode, whirling through the cielo gobbling a
    luna or two, he made a sacrifice to the double god
    Muerte.
An estrella.

Jean Morrison

Poems Using Spanish Words

Writing these poems enabled children who knew Spanish to enjoy their knowledge of it and gave those who didn't a feeling for another language. Other languages might be more to the point in other places: I chose Spanish because there were so many Spanish-speaking children in the school. I wanted their feelings for Spanish words to be part of their work, and I wanted to show them how knowing more than one language could be an advantage in writing poetry. Too often, the non-English language a child knows is regarded in school as something that has to be overcome rather than as an additional source of knowledge and pleasure. The non-Spanish-speaking students enjoyed the poem for the color, music, and strangeness of the Spanish words.

To help the children feel the difference between words in the two languages, I asked them to close their eyes while I said certain words such as "star" and "sky" in English and then in Spanish (*estrella, cielo*). I asked them what color each of the words was, which was more beautiful, which was softer, and so on.

Some children may feel awkward and embarrassed about using words in a language they don't know, so the poem should be made exciting and easy to write. The best idea I had was the one I used in the fifth-grade class. It was close to Christmas, so holidays were in the air. I asked the children to invent a new holiday and write a poem about it; the holiday should have new customs and ceremonies, new characters (like Santa Claus), and be in a new place. Since everything about it was new, it would need new words to describe it; and for these I asked them to use some of the Spanish words I would write on the board. Or, if they preferred, they could write the whole poem in Spanish. I had prepared a list of Spanish words I thought they might find exciting to use in describing a new holiday. I wrote on the board their English equivalents and asked for the Spanish translations. These were the words: *paloma* (dove); *carambano* (icicle); *rojo* (red); *azul* (blue); *violeta* (violet); *verde* (green); *amarillo* (yellow); *purpureo* (purple); *estrella* (star); *hombre* (man); *invierno* (winter); *culebra* (snake); *noche* (night); *león* (lion); *mono* (monkey); *fiesta* (holiday); *baile* (dance); *oso* (bear); *nieve* (snow); *árboles* (trees); *rosa* (rose); *fuegos artificiales* (fireworks); *plato* (dish); *mar* (sea).

While writing, many students asked me for other Spanish words: the word for "people," for "suit," and so on. My Spanish-English dictionary enabled me to answer some but not all of their questions. The errors in these poems are the result of the ones I couldn't answer. Ilona Baburka, for example, asked me how to say "dovey" in Spanish, and since I didn't know, she had to use simply "dove," that is, *"la paloma."* The same with "dancing," which in her poem should be *"bailantes,"* not *"baile."*

The rules for the poem in the other classes (third and fourth grades combined, sixth grade, and Mrs. Magnani's fifth grade) were simpler, and they left out the holiday. I put a list of Spanish words on the blackboard and asked the children to include one or two in each line.

Other Poems

Third Grade

Sad Things Happy Things

One of the saddest things are colors because colors are sad and
roses are sad two lips are sad and having dates is sad too
but the saddest color I know is orange because it is so
bright that it makes you cry.
One of the happiest colors are white, blue, yellow these colors
are so happy because they are bright too so colors are
really sad, happy, lovely, and sometimes laughing colors so
colors are really everything.

Mayra Morales

When I came to New York I was gay as the gray day
On the plane to New York was as blue as the sky
When I went to sleep on the plane everything was as black as
  my dress
I had pink shoes that were as pink as Marion's cheeks.

Ileana Mesen

A Dream

I went to sleep and had this dream.

I was going into an old house.
It was made of paper inside and made of candy outside.
When I saw the outside I wanted to go in.
When I went in I saw a window which was made of apples
  and roses.
There lived an old lady who was wearing a dress of wood.
She had some fruit on the table that was made of cream.
I sat on the chair and when I got up it was made of glue.
Then I woke up and my mother was the old lady.
And I never ate fruit again.

Mercedes Mesen

What Has Happened To Me

I was very sad like the color white
I wish I was gay like the color of yellow
I used to be as happy as a pig eating his food
But now I'm as sad as a sitting duck
I am very sad like the color of my hair
I used to be happy like the color of my skin
But now I am sad, sad as can be
I wish I was happy, happy like ropes
But now I'm as sad as a frog leaping into the water
I wish my dreams were happy like a purple king
But now I'm so sad like a bird in a tree.

Michael Freihofer

A Funny Trip

I wish I could go on
a funny trip and see
a sailboat of sinking water
I wish I could go on a funny trip
and see a dog of midnight
I wish I could go on a funny funny trip
and see a dress of shoes
I wish I could go on a funny funny trip
and hear a pocketful of laughs

Eliza Bailey

Third and Fourth Grades

Good-bye hospital hello grave
Good-bye blood hello death
Good-bye Miss Pilkington hello Mrs. Strasser
Good-bye noise hello quiet
Good-bye schoolwork hello homework
Good-bye fire hello water

Steven Lenik

Good-bye Mr. Chips hello Thomas Edison.
Good-bye explorers hello pioneers.
Good-bye rocks hello stones.
Good-bye games hello sports.
Good-bye people hello animals.

Mario Morales

Good-bye work hello play
Good-bye pop hello boys
Good-bye boyfriend hello another
Good-bye honeybun hello darling

Myrna Diaz

Hello, Good-bye

Hello Texas, good-bye New York.
Hello Moon, good-bye Earth.
Hello, world, good-bye 10th Street.
Hello farm, good-bye city.
Hello horse, good-bye car.
Good-bye numbers, hello penmanship.

Maria Gutierrez

Hello Europe, good-bye America,
Hello clean land, good-bye stinkland.
Hello books, good-bye comic books.
Hello work, good-bye play.
Hello new friends, good-bye old friends.

Alex Morrison

Good-bye crawling hello walking
Good-bye diapers hello panties
Good-bye hairy hello baldy

Melissa Blitz

Good-bye Maria, Hello Valerie,
Good-bye Valerie, Hello Leda,
Good-bye Leda, Hello John,
Good-bye Gary, Hello John,
Good-bye Carmen, Hello John,
Good-bye Lyn, Hello John,
Good-bye Robin, Hello John,
Good-bye Chip, Hello John,
Good-bye Mario, Hello John,
Good-bye Missy, Hello John,
And Good-bye John, Hello
TO THE GIRL HATERS
CLUB OF AMERICA
And Good-bye John.

Markus Niebanck

Fourth Grade

Things Around Central Park

What are big things with eyes?
They are buildings with windows.
What are big pointy pencils?
They are really steeples on a church.
What are big green lollipops?
They are big green trees.
What is a big green full of people place?
That is Central Park.

Martin Freihofer

To Mrs. Wiener
Crunching a pretzel
Waiting for the afternoon
When somebody will give her another
You can see how she likes it
Taking extremely large pieces
We should name this poem
Mrs. Wiener and the Pretzel

Annie Clayton

An Animal Garden

An animal garden
Is what it is
Something like mine
At my house
But it probably has
More animals.
But still, you can't
Be sure.
Mine has seventy-two
But Central Park's zoo
Has bigger ones.
I have lions and ducks
But no skunks
Just one camel
Lots of cats
Many frogs
But Central Park
Has no dinosaurs.
But my animals
Are just toys
Except two of the cats.

Erin Harold

New York City

New York, N. Y. is a busy city
You have to run to catch your show
You walk the black cat's eyes
You breathe the pollutioned air
You catch a bouncing bus
You bounce all the way home
You open the cat's eyelid with your key.
You walk inside the cat's tail.
You catch a house
In your hand and swallow it down.
I hate New York and every book
Because when you open a book,
Here it is you catch the world and
Roar, Roar, Roar and Roar

Socorrito Caballero

Sixth Grade

Assassination

A victory is achieved
But a great loss is just ahead
In a pantry of a hotel
Eight shots rang out like firecrackers
R.F.K. lies mortally wounded
Three shots plowed through his strong body.
Beneath him is a pool of blood
Oh my dear god, is he dead?
That night was a night of praying
But his state is still critical.
He has lived through a day of suffering
But that night his great life disappeared.

Roberto Marcilla

Other Poems

I included this section to suggest the variety of themes children can write poems about. These were written in response to topics proposed by me and by several P.S. 61 teachers: an exciting experience; happy things and sad things, using colors; hello and good-bye; an imitation of William Carlos Williams (Annie Clayton's poem); New York City; Central Park; the assassination of Robert Kennedy.

The Central Park poems were the result of an outing there by the fourth-grade class. I suggested they write two poems—one while they were in Central Park, one afterwards. Having a class write poems outside school is something I want to do more of: in zoos, in museums, on the banks of a river, any place interesting and exciting. The children can be helped, just as they are inside school, by suggestions: beginning every line with "If I were a monkey," a poem about why you like the twentieth-century world better than Ancient Egypt or vice versa, a poem about what you would do if you were a river.